Computer Applications Exam Success

Do not be Afraid of Exams,
Study these Papers and Score Good Marks

by

BPB Editorial Board

FIRST EDITION 2020

ISBN: 978-93-89845-020

Distributors:

BPB PUBLICATIONS
20, Ansari Road, Darya Ganj
New Delhi-110002
Ph: 23254990/23254991

DECCAN AGENCIES
4-3-329, Bank Street,
Hyderabad-500195
Ph: 24756967/24756400

MICRO MEDIA
Shop No. 5, Mahendra Chambers,
150 DN Rd. Next to Capital Cinema,
V.T. (C.S.T.) Station, MUMBAI-400 001
Ph: 22078296/22078297

BPB BOOK CENTRE
376 Old Lajpat Rai Market,
Delhi-110006
Ph: 23861747

Published by Manish Jain for BPB Publications, 20 Ansari Road, Darya Ganj, New Delhi-110002

Preface

With the recent revision of the syllabus, the CBSE has changed the marking scheme and the exam pattern. All this has been kept in mind while writing this book. The book in your hand is strictly based on the new CBSE syllabus and promises to deliver the content keeping in mind the learning outcomes of the subject.

The papers are divided into four Sections - Section A and B has to be attempted by all students, whereas the students may attempt any one of the Two sections from Section C or Section D.

Errata

We take immense pride in our work at BPB Publications and follow best practices to ensure the accuracy of our content to provide with an indulging reading experience to our subscribers. Our readers are our mirrors, and we use their inputs to reflect and improve upon human errors if any, occurred during the publishing processes involved. To let us maintain the quality and help us reach out to any readers who might be having difficulties due to any unforeseen errors, please write to us at :

errata@bpbonline.com

Your support, suggestions and feedbacks are highly appreciated by the BPB Publications' Family.

Table of Contents

SAMPLE
PAPER
2019-20

Computer Application (CBSE) Code-165

Sample Question Paper 2019-20

M.M. 30 **Time: 2 hrs**

General instructions

- **This paper contains 4 sections-Section A, Section B, Section C, and Section D.**
- **Section A and B has to be attempted by all students.**
- **Students may attempt any one of the two sections from Section C (Scratch) and Section D (Python).**

SECTION 'A' (7 Marks)

1. Expand SMTP. **(1)**

2. Consider the following HTML statement:

```
<body bgcolor="Blue" alink ="red" vlink="yellow">
```

In the above statement, what do you mean by 'alink' and 'vlink'? **(1)**

3. Rashmi has to send an email to Raees. She also wants to send the same e-mail to Vandana but does not want Raees to know about it. Which option out of '*cc*' or '*bcc*' should Rashmi use to enter the e-mail address of Vandana? **(1)**

4. Geetu is an artist. She posts her artwork on the internet. One day she comes to know that Shreyas has downloaded one of the paintings that she had posted without her permission. He had further printed that image on an invitation card. Has Shreyas done the right thing? Which right of Geetu has he infringed?

OR

Define plagiarism. **(1)**

5. Give one difference between 3G and 4G. **(1)**

6. Define the term Digital Divide. **(1)**

7. Ritwik wants to use a software but does not want to pay for it. Which type of software can he use? **(1)**

SECTION 'B' **(15 Marks)**

8. Write any one application each of e-Governance and e-commerce. **(2)**

9. Kuhu has just learnt how to do online banking. Name any two precautions that she should take to prevent online fraud. **(2)**

10. Name the following with respect to HTML: **(2)**

    a. Attribute for changing bullet type of list tag.

    b. Element to create a hyperlink

11. Write HTML code to display the unordered list (with square bullets) of two cities "DELHI" and "MUMBAI". The web page should have a yellow background and the title of the page should be 'My Cities.'

    OR

    Write HTML code to display an ordered list (with uppercase roman numbers) listing any three subjects being taught in your school. The web page should have a red background and the title of the page should be 'My Subjects' **(2)**

12. Form a CSS code within the `<head>...</head>`, for the following specifications:
    Background colour: blue for the paragraph,
    font family is Dotum and colour of the text is red,
    Heading should be in black colour. **(2)**

13. Write the HTML code to do the following: **(2)**

    a. To display a horizontal line of green colour.

    b. To create a hyperlink on the word CLICK to an image named testimage. jpeg

14. Write output of the following HTML code.

```
<html>
<head>
<title> Table </title>
</head>
<body>
<table border="1">
<tr>
```

```
<td align="center" rowspan="2"> ONE </td>
<td> TWO </td>
<td>THREE</td>
</tr>
<tr>
<td> Rose </td>
<td> Lily </td>
</tr>
<tr>
<td align="center"> Pansy </td>
<td align="center" colspan="2"> Dahlia</td>
</tr>
</table>
</body>
</html>
```

OR

Observe the following table and write the HTML code to generate it: **(3)**

SERIALNO	CLASS	NUMBER OF STUDENTS		
		ENGLISH	HINDI	REGIONAL
1	X A	35	10	6
2	X B	31	15	4

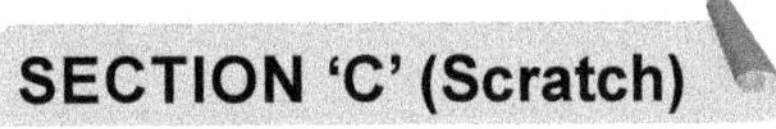

SECTION 'C' (Scratch) **(8 Marks)**

15.  Differentiate between 

and 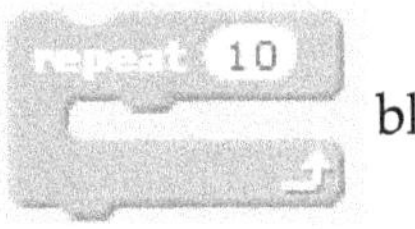

blocks?

OR

Differentiate between 

and if then else blocks. **(2)**

16. Study the scripts given below and answer the questions. **(4)**

(*i*) What will be the final position of the cat (Scratch mascot) after running the following script? **(1)**

```
when [flag] clicked
clear
glide 3 secs to x: 90 y: 90
turn ↻ 15 degrees
glide 5 secs to x: 0 y: 0
```

(*ii*) What happens when the sprite does not touch the edge of the stage? **(1)**

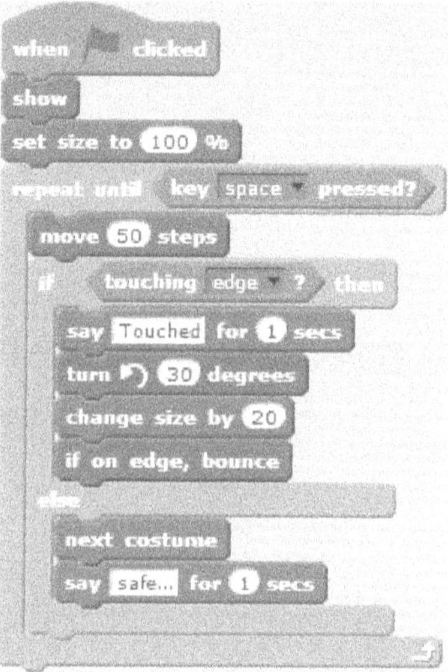

(*iii*) In question (*ii*) above, what happens when the sprite touches the edges. **(2)**

17. Name the tab and category of blocks that should be selected to do the following: **(2)**

(*i*) Ask the user's name

(*ii*) Add a variable to store points of the game

SECTION 'D' (Python) **(8 Marks)**

18. Which of the following are valid variable names in Python?

`1plus2, if, my_book, yes&no, helloworld1`

19. What will be output of the following expressions?

```
#Considering Python 2.7
>>> print ('Test' * 3)
>>> print ('7'+'8')
```

OR

```
#Considering Python 3.x
>>> print ('Test' * 3)
>>> print ('7'+'8')
```

(2)

20. What will be output of the following code if the user enters Principal amount as 20000 and Time as 10 years.

```
#Considering Python 2.7
P = input("Enter Principal amount:")
T = input("Enter Time:")
if T>10:
SI = P*T*10/100
else:
SI = P*T*15/100
print("Simple Interest = ",SI)
```

OR

```
#Considering Python 3.x
P = input("Enter Principal amount:")
T = input("Enter Time:")
if T>10:
SI = P*T*10/100
else:
SI = P*T*15/100
print("Simple Interest = ",SI)
```

(2)

21. Write a code that displays the sum of first 10 natural numbers. (3)

For Solutions of the above Sample Paper

Go to: https://qrgo.page.link/BBbGG Or Scan:

Extra
Bytes

Connecting to a Website

Each digital communication involves a request from the client, and a response from the server. The format and content of each message is determined by the communication protocol, which is agreed upon the devices used in advance.

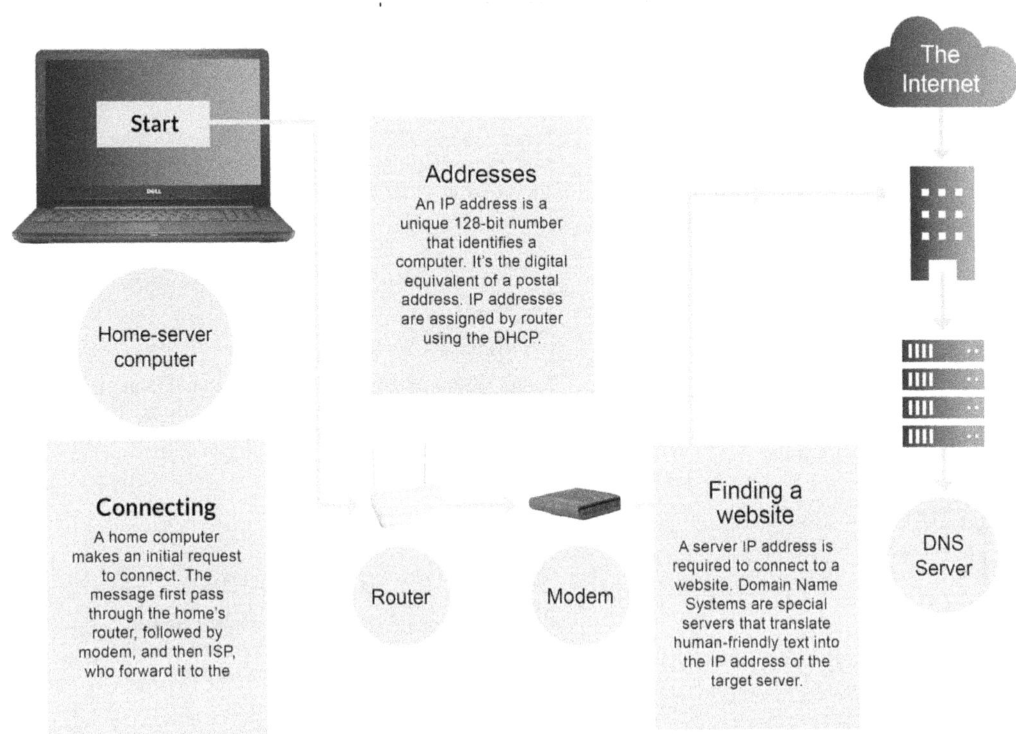

Social media platforms

A social media platform is an online place where communities can gather to make connections and share user-generated content. There are different types of social media platform.

1978
Bulletin Boards

1985
The WELL

1996
ICQ

2000
TripAdvisor

2002
Friendster Last.fm

2003
LinkedIn

2004
Digg , Vimeo , Yelp , Facebook

2005
Reddit , Youtube

2006
Goodreads , Twitter

2007
Tumbler

2010
Quora

2011
Snapchat

Discussion forums

These are crowd-run sites where the community determines the tone, regulations, and which subjects are up for discussion.

Online Review

These platforms allow people to post their thoughts about everything from dentists to restaurants, to help others choose where to go and what to do.

Social media Platforms

Personal relationship networks connect people. Professional networks connect current or future colleagues. Dating networks connect people romantically.

Media-sharing networks

Social media-sharing networks let user publish videos, images and audio, and connect users with audiences and collaborators.

Digital Property Right

Digital property is the property which is created by you online or digitally. This property may be in terms of your own creation, picture, art, music, video clips etc.

How to view the HTML of a website

It's possible to view the HTML of any page on the web. The HTML of bigger websites are optimized and can be quite difficult to understand. However, if smaller websites are checked, some of the details may be recognizable.

Explanation of CSS in pictorial form

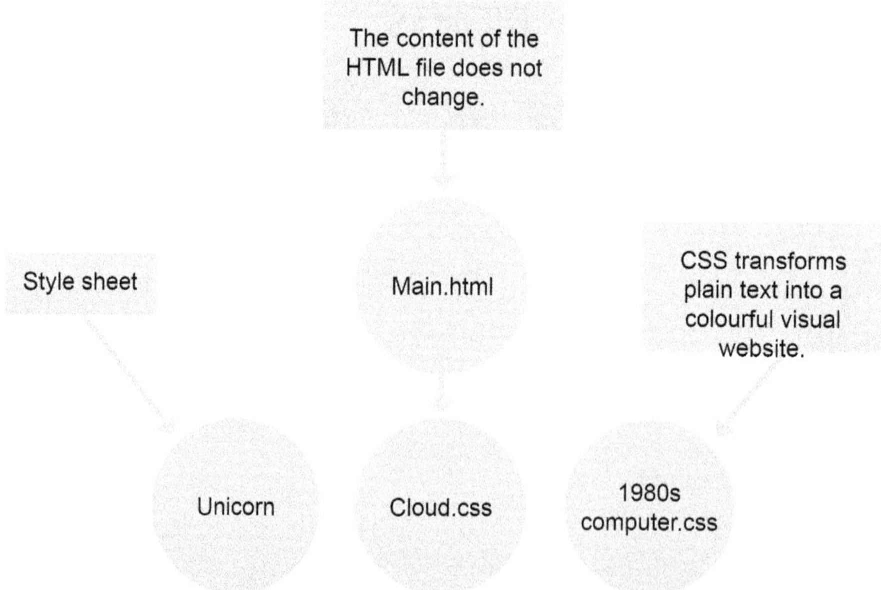

Installing and launching scratch

To start programming in Scratch, you need to have the Scratch software. It can be installed on a computer, or it can be used online.

Online

once you have joined the Scratch website, click Sig in and enter user name and password. click Create at the top of the screen to begin a new program.

When you are logged in, Scratch automatically saves work for you.

The web version of Scratch works well on Windows, Ubuntu and Mac Computer.

Offline

Double-click the icon on the desktop and scratch will scratch.

Click the File menu at the top of the screen and choose Save As. Ask the person who owns the computer where you should save your work.

The offline version of Scratch works well on Windows and Mac computers.

Step 1: Launching Scratch

Step 2: Saving Work

Step 3: Operating Systems

Planning Programs in Python

When you are writing code with lots of branches, its worth planning out what will happen on each branch. This helps you keep track of what's going on, so you end up with fewer errors in your code.

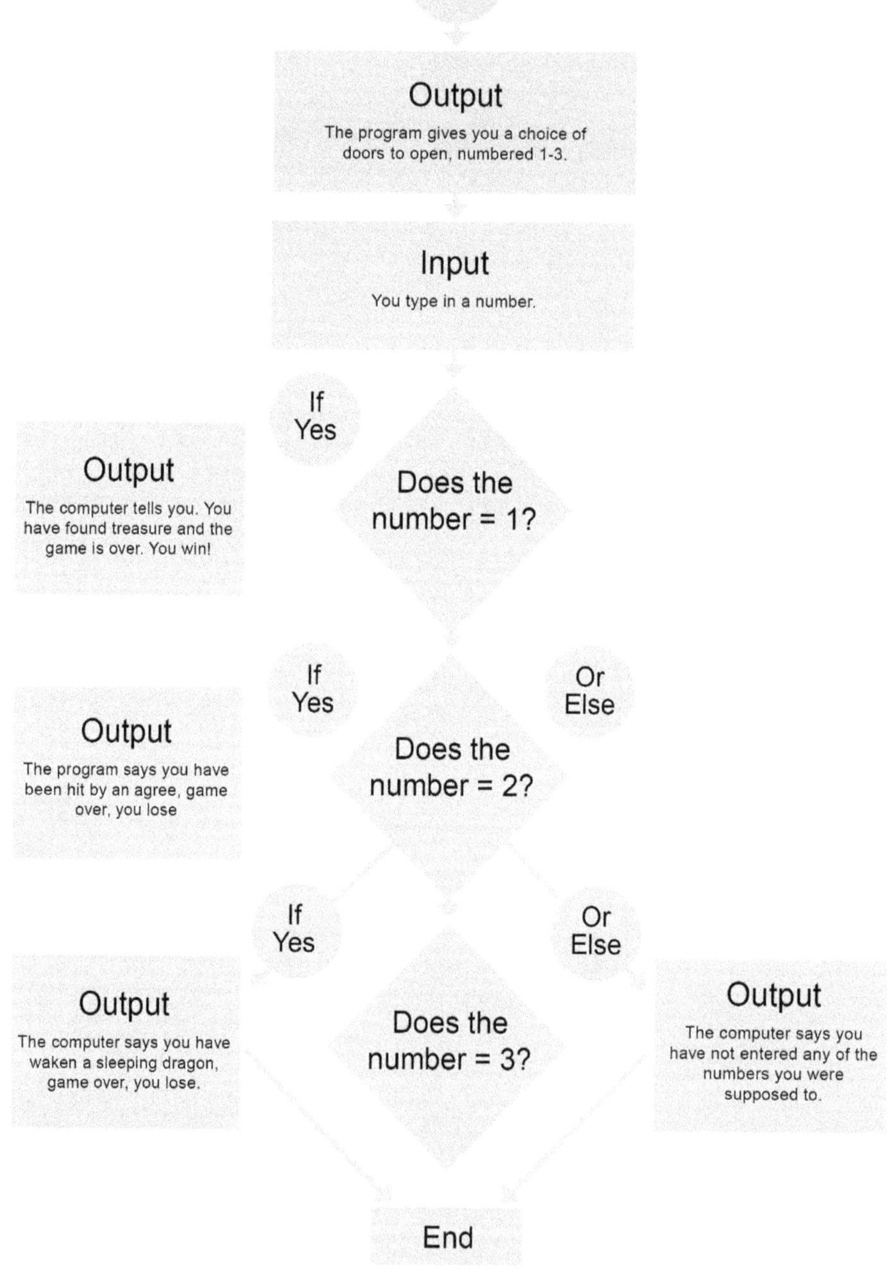

SAMPLE
PAPERS

Computer Application (CBSE) Code-165

Sample Question Paper 1

M.M. 30 **Time: 2 hrs**

General instructions

- **This paper contains 4 sections-Section A, Section B, Section C, and Section D.**
- **Section A and B has to be attempted by all students.**
- **Students may attempt any one of the two sections from Section C (Scratch) and Section D (Python).**

SECTION 'A' (7 Marks)

1. Expand WWW. (1)
2. Which tag is used to insert the link? (1)
3. Name the parts that are separated by the @ sign in an e-mail address. (1)
4. What is the use of the open source software? (1)
5. Why do you use a web browser? (1)
6. What do you mean by cyber fraud? (1)
7. Define online reservation. (1)

SECTION 'B' (15 Marks)

8. What is the difference between the Cc and Bcc fields? (2)
9. How to install a firewall? (2)
10. Explain the command: `<A HREF="auto.HTML">` Click here for `autobiography</A>`. (2)
11. Consider the given HTML code and answer the following: (2)

```
<A HREF=#intro> Introduction </A>
```

In the above code:

a. What is the purpose of the #?

b. What will happen when the user clicks on `Introduction`?

OR

What is the purpose of using the `VALIGN` attribute in tables?

12. What are the limits of the text field size? **(2)**

13. Consider the following webpage: **(2)**

a. Identify how many times the `<BR>` tag are used in this web page.

b. Is the `<BR>` tag an empty tag? If yes, please explain.

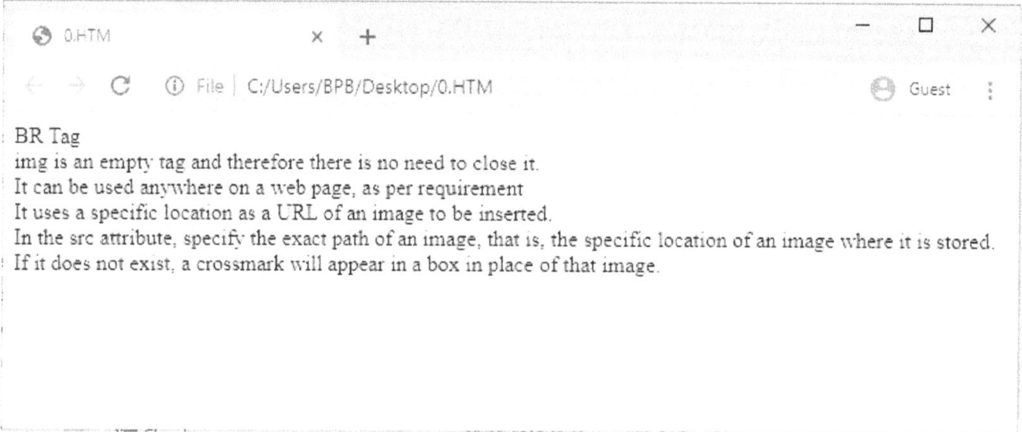

14. Observe the following table and write the HTML code to generate it: **(3)**

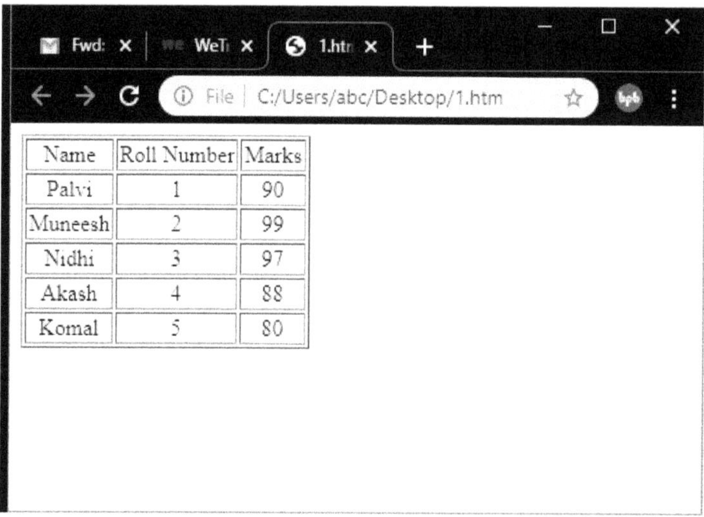

Name	Roll Number	Marks
Palvi	1	90
Muneesh	2	99
Nidhi	3	97
Akash	4	88
Komal	5	80

OR

Write the HTML code to demonstrate the ordered and unordered list. Note that the ordered items are **Yellow** in color and the unordered items are **Aqua** in color.

SECTION 'C' (Scratch) **(8 Marks)**

15. Write down the names and function of three tempo blocks. **(2)**

OR

What is the difference between the `Repeat()` block and repeat `until()` block.

16. Draw a Pentagon using the repeat block of commands. **(4)**

17. What is the use of : **(2)**

a. when clicked

b. forever

SECTION 'D' (Python) **(8 Marks)**

18. Write down two rules for declaring identifiers. **(1)**

19. Find the output of the following code fragments: **(2)**

```
num1,num2,num3=4,5,6
print(num1,num2,num3)
```

20. Find the error from the following code: **(3)**

```
a=William
b=smith
Print a+b
```

21. Write a program to enter the minutes and convert it into hours and minutes.

Answers

SECTION 'A'

1. WWW stands for World Wide Web. It is a global network of computers using the internet to exchange web documents.
2. The anchor <A> tag is used to insert the link.
3. The two main parts are the username and the hostname.
4. It can be modified or enhanced for the reusability and accessibility of a program.
5. It is used for accessing and retrieving information from the internet.
6. A fraud committed online is known as cyber fraud, online fraud, internet fraud or simply fraud.
7. It is the process of reserving the tickets via the internet.

SECTION 'B'

8. Cc: It refers to the Carbon Copy field. The recipients whose e-mail addresses are added in the Cc field would receive a copy of the mail.

   Bcc: It refers to the Blind Carbon Copy field. The recipients whose e-mail addresses are added in the Bcc field would receive a copy of the mail. However, the identity of these recipients would not be disclosed.
9. A firewall is a program or hardware device that filters the information coming through an internet connection to a network or a computer system. If incoming information does not pass the rules stored in the firewall, it is not allowed to pass through.
10. This command will open the `auto.HTML` web page in the browser when we click the hypertext -`Click` here for `autobiography`.
11. *a.* The # symbol is used to tell the Web browser that this link is in the same Web page.

    b. When we click on `Introduction`, we are redirected (or sent) to the section named `intro`, in the web page.

OR

The `VALIGN` attribute vertically aligns the data in a table. It is used with the `<TD>` tag. The `VALIGN` attribute takes three values - top, middle and bottom.

It is used when there is a span of two or more than two rows, and we have to align the data vertically either at the top, middle or the bottom.

12. The default size for a text field is around 13 characters. However, if we include the size attribute, we can set the size value to be as low as 1. The maximum size value will be determined by the browser width. If the size attribute is set to 0, the size will be set to the default size of 13 characters.

13. a.
 tag is used four times.

b. The <BR> tag is an empty tag because it has no end tag.

14. Refer to the following HTML code:

```
<HTML>
<HEAD>
</HEAD>
<BODY>
<TABLE BORDER= "1" WIDTH = "210">
<TR ALIGN= "CENTER">
<TD> Name</TD>
<TD>Roll Number</TD>
<TD> Marks</TD>
</TR>
<TR ALIGN= "CENTER">
<TD>Palvi</TD>
<TD>1</TD>
<TD>90</TD>
</TR>
<TR ALIGN= "CENTER">
<TD>Muneesh</TD>
<TD>2</TD>
<TD>99</TD>
</TR>
<TR ALIGN= "CENTER">
<TD>Nidhi</TD>
<TD>3</TD>
<TD>97</TD>
```

```
</TR>
<TR ALIGN= "CENTER">
<TD>Akash</TD>
<TD>4</TD>
<TD>88</TD>
</TR>
<TR ALIGN= "CENTER">
<TD>Komal</TD>
<TD>5</TD>
<TD>80</TD>
</TR>
</TABLE>
</BODY>
</HTML>
```

OR

Refer to the following code:

```
<HTML>
<HEAD>
</HEAD>
<BODY>
<OL>
<FONT COLOR = "Yellow">
<LI> Names </LI>
<LI> Roll Number </LI>
<LI> Marks </LI>
</OL>
<UL>
<FONT COLOR = "Aqua">
<LI> Square </LI>
<LI> Circle </LI>
<LI> Rectangle </LI>
</UL>
</BODY>
</HTML>
```

SECTION 'C' (Scratch)

15. Refer to the following table:

Block	Function
tempo	Reports the value of the current tempo.
change tempo by 20	Changes the tempo by a specified value.
set tempo to 60 bpm	Sets the tempo to a given value.

OR

The `Repeat ()` block is a Control block and a C block. The blocks held inside this block will loop a given amount of times, before allowing the script to continue. The `RepeatUntil ()` block is a Control block and a C block. The blocks held inside this block will loop until the specified Boolean statement is true, in which case, the code beneath the block (if any) will execute. This loop is similar to a while loop in some other programming languages.

16. To draw a pentagon,

a. Pen must be in drawing position.

b. Point in Right direction.

c. Repeat following commands 5 times:

i. Move 100 steps.

ii. Turn 360/5 degrees.

```
when [flag] clicked
clear
pen down
point in direction 90
repeat 5
    move 100 steps
    turn ↶ 360 / 5 degrees
```

17. *a.* The when clicked block starts the execution of script.

b. The forever block is used to perform a task repeatedly.

SECTION 'D' (Python)

18. The rules for declaring the identifiers are:

    a. An identifier should not be a keyword.

    b. An identifier should not begin with a digit.

19. `4 5 6`

20.
```
a=”William”

b=”smith”

print(a+b)
```

21.
```
m=int(input(“Enter minutes : “))
h=m//60
m=m%60
print(“Hours=”,h)
print(“Minutes=”,m)
```

Computer Application (CBSE) Code-165

Sample Question Paper 2

M.M. 30 **Time: 2 hrs**

General instructions

- **This paper contains 4 sections-Section A, Section B, Section C, and Section D.**
- **Section A and B has to be attempted by all students.**
- **Students may attempt any one of the two sections from Section C (Scratch) and Section D (Python).**

SECTION 'A' (7 Marks)

1. List down the freely available video conferencing software. **(1)**
2. Name the different attributes used with form tag. **(1)**
3. What is the use of SSH? **(1)**
4. What do you mean by e-groups? **(1)**

   OR

   Write down one advantage of online shopping.
5. How can you make a strong password? **(1)**
6. What does a non-profit organization specify? **(1)**
7. What do you mean by freedom of information? **(1)**

SECTION 'B' (15 Marks)

8. Sidharth wants to study online and he asked his friend about the same. How can he achieve his goal? Mention its benefits also. **(2)**
9. Nishi is a student of `Class-X` and she has to prepare notes on cybercrimes. For this purpose, she explored the topic from the internet and copied information from there without citing it or putting it in quotation marks. **(2)**

   a. What kind of cybercrime would this be?

b. How can you avoid this?

10. Name the following with respect to external linking. **(2)**

a. Write down the syntax for creating an external linking.

b. Name the attribute that is used for external linking.

11. Explain the attributes of `<img>` tag. **(2)**

OR

What do you mean by form controls? Name the different type of form controls.

12. Write down the HTML code for the following: **(2)**

a. To insert an image in JPG.

b. To display the image in the center, with height 100 and width 100.

13. Observe the following HTML image and write a code to generate it. **(3)**

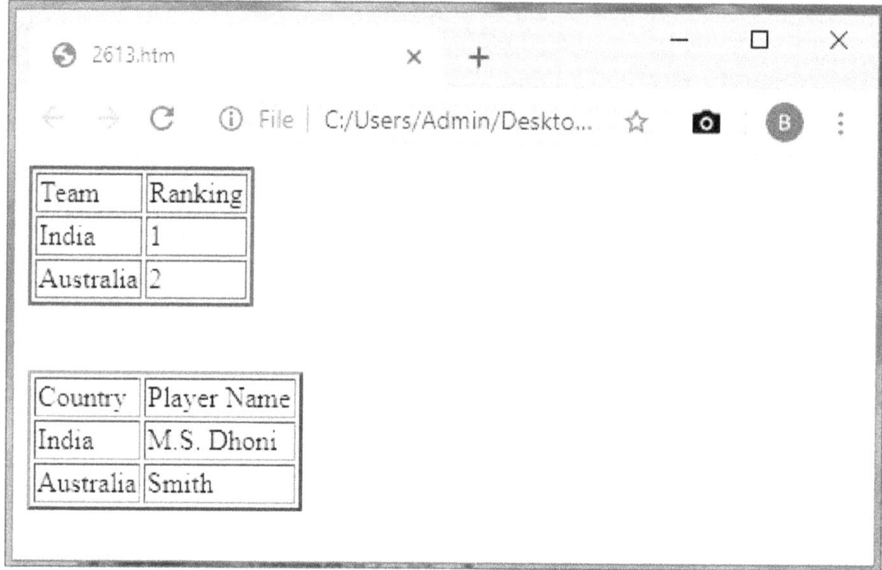

Team	Ranking
India	1
Australia	2

Country	Player Name
India	M.S. Dhoni
Australia	Smith

OR

Write the output of the following code.

```
<HTML>
<BODY>
<TABLE border ="1" height="50%">
<TR>
```

```
<TH>Spring</TH>
<TH>Summer</TH>
<TH>Winter</TH>
</TR>
<TR>
<TD>Orchid</TD>
<TD>Galdiolus</TD>
<TD>Rose</TD>
</TR>
<TR>
<TD>Lilly</TD>
<TD>Lilac</TD>
<TD>Cyclamen</TD>
</TR>
<TR>
<TD>Tulip</TD>
<TD>Freesia</TD>
<TD>Amaryllis</TD>
</TR>
</TABLE>
</BODY>
</HTML>
```

SECTION 'C' (Scratch) (8 Marks)

14. What is the use of motion block in scratch? **(1)**

OR

What do you mean by backdrop?

15. Explain the commands of Pen block. **(4)**

16. Draw a triangle using the repeat block of commands. **(3)**

SECTION 'D' (Python) (8 Marks)

17. What is Python and who developed it? **(1)**

18. Assuming `num = 125`, determine the value of each of the following Python expressions: **(2)**

    a. `num/125`

    b. `num%100`

    c. `(num==21) & (2<3)`

    d. `Not((num<45.9)& (6*2<=13))`

19. Write the output of the following program lines. **(2)**

    a. `print("Hello" *3)`

    b. `print("Hello"+"Welcome")`

20. Write a program in Python to find the volume of a sphere. **(3)**

Answers

SECTION 'A'

1. Some freely available video conferencing software are TCPCam, Ekiga or GnomeMeeting, Skype for Linux, Brosix, and Goober.
2. The various attributes used with form tag are action, method, and name.
3. SSH is widely used by network administrators for managing systems and applications remotely.
4. E-groups are a list of e-mails, users that can share information among each other.

    OR

    Providing the users with the facility of shopping from any trader and at any time, is an advantage of online shopping.
5. A password that is longer than 10 characters, having a combination of upper and lower-case letters, digits and at least one special character, usually makes a strong password.
6. It specifies a website created for non-profit ventures, such as http:// www.quora.com.
7. Freedom of information refers to the freedom of speech, accessing information through the internet, sharing the relevant information with each other, discussing various topics on social media, and so on.

SECTION 'B'

8. He should use the concept of e-learning. It is learning with the help of electronic resources like computers, tablets, smart phones, and the internet.

9. *a.* Since Nishi copied the article from internet without citing it or using quotation marks, is known as plagiarism.

   b. It can be avoided by citing the name of the person who wrote the article, or she should write this article on her own.

10. *a.* The syntax for creating an external link is:

```
<A href="URL">Text to be displayed</A>
```

   b. For external linking, use the HREF attribute with the <A> tag,which will specify the URL of the document to be linked.

11. Refer to the following table:

Attribute	Value	Description
Src	URL	Specifies the URL of an image.
Alt	Text	Specifies an alternate text for an image.
Align	Top, bottom, middle, left, right	Specifies the alignment of an image, according to surrounding elements.
Border	Pixels	Specifies the width of the border around an image.
Height	Pixels	Specifies the height of an image.
Width	Pixels	Specifies the width of an image.

OR

A form is a window that consists of the elements of a form, called the form fields. These fields are also known as form controls.

The different types of form controls are text field, text area, dropdown box, radio buttons, checkbox, password field, select, and/or a command button.

12. Refer to the following code:

```
<HTML>
<body>
<center>
<img src="mytree.jpg" alt="Trees are life" width="500"
height="500" ></center>
</body>
```

```
</HTML>
```

13. Refer to the following code:

```
<HTML>
<HEAD><TITLE></TITLE></HEAD>
<BODY>
<TABLE border = “2” bordercolor=”Red”>
<TR>
<TD> Team </TD>
<TD> Ranking </TD>
</TR>
<TR>
<TD> India </TD>
<TD>1   </TD>
</TR>
<TR>
<TD> Australia </TD>
<TD>2  </TD>
</TR>
</TABLE>
<br><br>
<TABLE border = “2”>
<TR>
<TD> Country</TD>
<TD> Player Name </TD>
</TR>
<TR>
<TD> India </TD>
<TD> M.S. Dhoni  </TD>
</TR>
<TR>
<TD> Australia </TD>
<TD>Smith  <Smith </TD>
</TR>
```

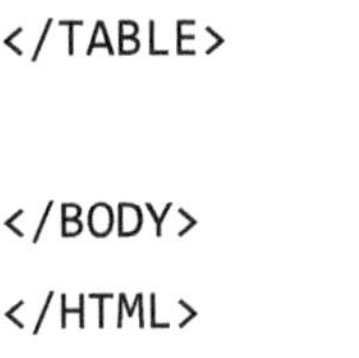

```
</TABLE>

</BODY>
</HTML>
```

OR

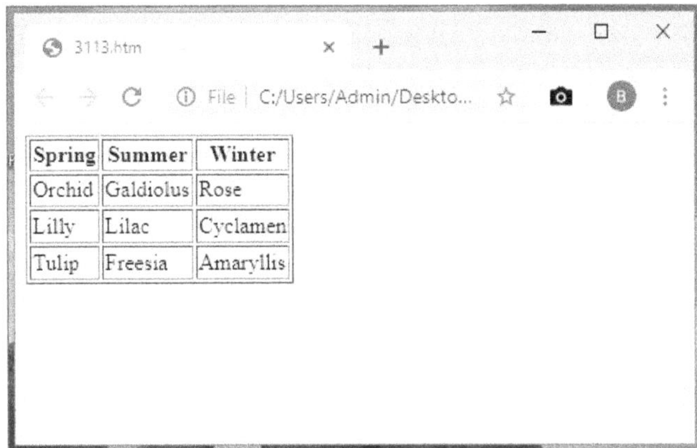

Spring	Summer	Winter
Orchid	Galdiolus	Rose
Lilly	Lilac	Cyclamen
Tulip	Freesia	Amaryllis

SECTION 'C' (Scratch)

14. It controls the movement of sprites. It changes the angle of the movement of a sprite according to X-axis and Y-axis.

OR

All the action in a scratch game takes place on a stage. Sprites can move around on the stage, often in front of a background image, which is called a backdrop.

15. Refer to the following points:

a. clear : It clears the drawings created by all the sprites. It has no effect on the stage background.

b. stamp : It causes the sprite image (the current costume) to be stamped as a stamp image.

c. pen down : It causes the pen to be applied. The movements performed will cause a drawing to be created in accordance with the pen settings (color, thickness).

d. pen up : It causes the pen to be raised. Sprite movements will not result in the creation of a drawing.

e. set pen color to : It sets the Pen's color based on the choice from the color picker.

f. change pen color by 10 : It changes the Pen's color by the specified amount.

g. set pen color to 0 : It sets the Pen's color by the specified amount.

h. change pen shade by 10 : It changes the Pen's shade by the specified amount.

i. set pen shade to 50 : It sets the Pen's shade by the specified amount.

j. change pen size by 1 : It changes the thickness of the pen.

k. set pen size to 1 : It sets the thickness of the pen.

16. To draw a triangle:

a. The pen must be in the drawing position(pen down).

b. It should point in the right direction(value 90).

c. To draw a triangle, repeat the following commands 3 times:

i. Move 100 steps.

ii. Turn 120 degrees.

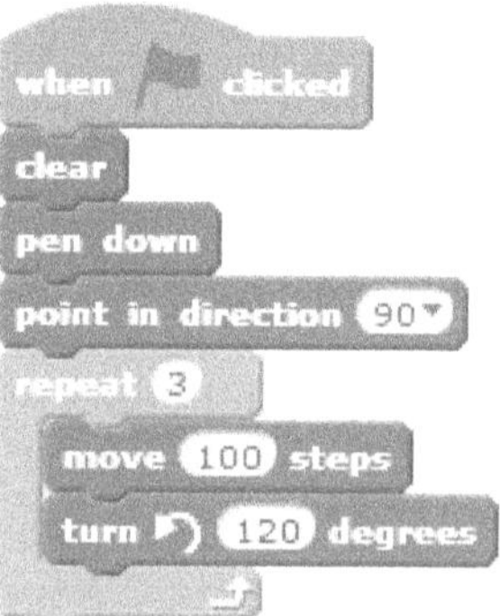

SECTION 'D' (Python)

17. Python is a high-level object-oriented language. It was developed by Guido Van Rosssum, during 1955-1990.

18. Refer to the following answers:

a. 1

b. 25

c. False

d. True

19. *a.* `HelloHelloHello`

b. `HelloWelcome`

20. Refer to the following code:

```
r=float(input("Enter radius : "))
pi = 3.14
r= 6.0
V= (4.0/3.0)*pi* (r**3)
print("The volume of the sphere is:",V)
```

Computer Application (CBSE) Code-165

Sample Question Paper 3

M.M. 30 **Time: 2 hrs**

General instructions

- **This paper contains 4 sections-Section A, Section B, Section C, and Section D.**
- **Section A and B has to be attempted by all students.**
- **Students may attempt any one of the two sections from Section C (Scratch) and Section D (Python).**

SECTION 'A' (7 Marks)

1. Write down the function of FTP. **(1)**
2. What is the purpose of the `<caption>` tag? **(1)**
3. Explain one feature of the OOS. **(1)**
4. What is a website and how it is related to hyperlink? **(1)**

   OR

   Name the devices that are used to connect to the internet.
5. What is Cyber Netiquette? **(1)**
6. Give the full form of the following: **(1)**
   a. URL
   b. SSH
7. Why is shareware not identical to open source software or free software? **(1)**

SECTION 'B' (15 Marks)

8. Sidharth has a leather business. Very often, he requires information from the internet about the latest developments in leather technology around the world. So, he wants an internet connection for his desktop computer. **(2)**

a. Suggest any two popular internet service providers in India.

b. Suggest two websites that could help him search for required information.

9. While transferring data, SSL encrypts it. What does it mean? **(2)**

10. Name the following with respect to HTML: **(2)**

a. What are the various types of image alignment?

b. The following code is written to align the image in the center of the browser's window. However, the desired result is not achieved. Mention the reason.

```
<IMG SRC="house.gif " ALIGN= "center">
```

11. Which form elements have been used to create controls having labels such as "`Login Id`", "`Classes`", "`Course Type`", and "`Submit`" as shown in the following screenshot of the "`e-Learning Member's Registration Page`". Also mention, how the form element given for the "`Classes`" is different from the form element given for the "`Course Type`". **(2)**

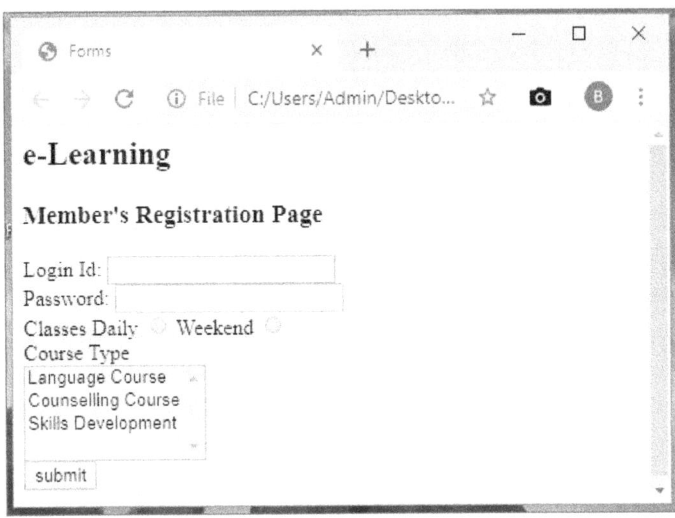

OR

Muneesh wants to send highly sensitive form data, like the username and password. Which method out of the GET/POST should he use to send the form data? Why?

12. Which tag is used to insert the link? Name the attribute that is mandatory for linking. **(2)**

13. Write the HTML code to display an image on the center side of the page. **(2)**

14. Observe the following code and answer the questions that follow: **(3)**

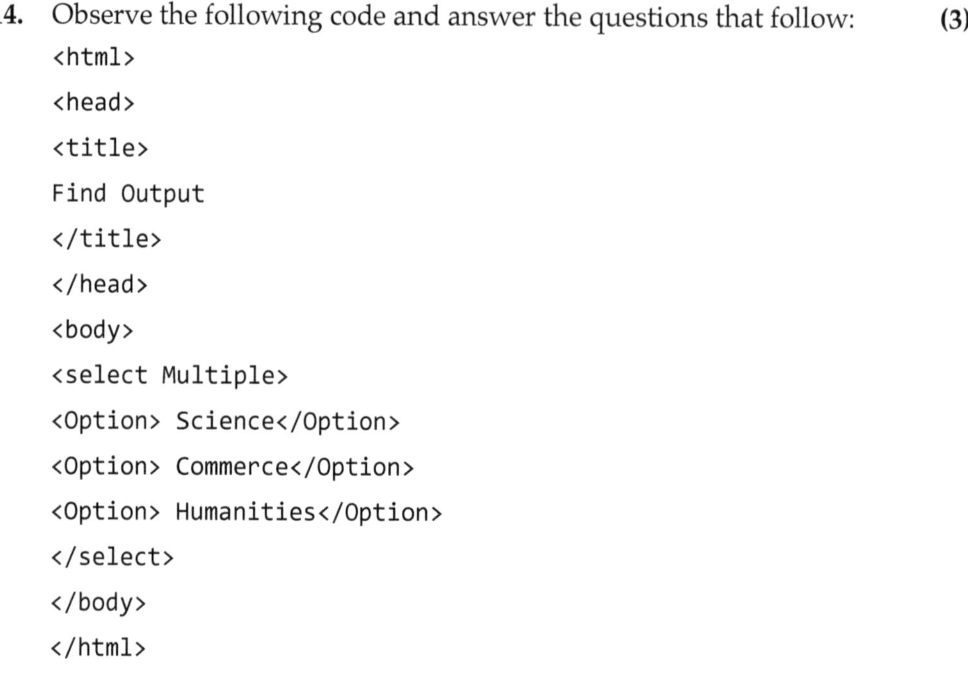

```
<html>
<head>
<title>
Find Output
</title>
</head>
<body>
<select Multiple>
<Option> Science</Option>
<Option> Commerce</Option>
<Option> Humanities</Option>
</select>
</body>
</html>
```

a. What is the use of the <select> tag in the above code?

b. Explain the purpose of the multiple attributes of the <select> tag.

OR

Write the HTML code for the given output:

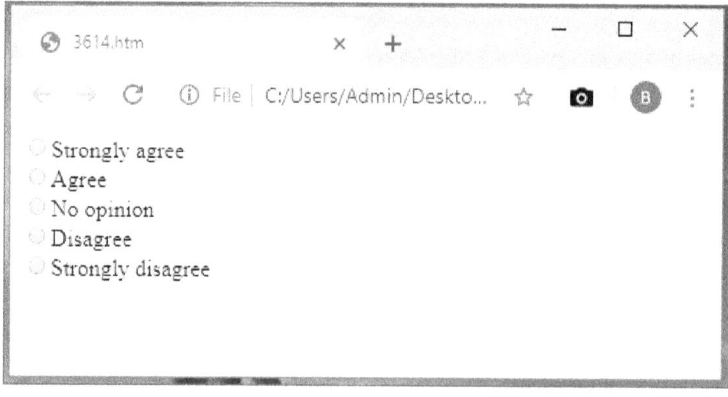

SECTION 'C' (Scratch) **(8 Marks)**

15. What is the purpose of the  block in Scratch? **(2)**

OR

What is the difference between the operator block and the sensor block?

16. Explain the different block shapes. **(4)**

17. How could you increase the game's time limit to 40 seconds? **(2)**

SECTION 'D' (Python) (8 Marks)

18. What is the significance of using the `range()` function? **(1)**

19. Consider the following code fragment and find the output: **(2)**

```
x = “abcdef”
i = “a”
while i in x:
    x = x[-6:-1]
print(i, end = “ “)
```

20. What will be the output of the following program segment? **(2)**

a.
```
a=5
a=25+4-4
print(a)
```

b.
```
a,b=0,30
a=30/2*b
print(a)
```

21. Write a program in Python to find the factorial of a number. **(3)**

Answers

SECTION 'A'

1. FTP is used for transmitting and sharing files over the internet.

2. The <caption> tag is used to provide a text to the table so that the contents of the table can be explained. It is generally in bold and at the center with respect to the table.

3. The user can fix the bugs, improve the functions, or adapt the software to suit their own needs.

(Answer may vary)

4. A website is a collection of several web pages, which are related with each other through a hyperlink.

OR

The following devices are required for connecting to the internet:

a. Computer

b. Modem

c. Transmission medium

d. Network Interface Card

e. Internet Service Provider (ISP)

5. Netiquette is short form of Internet Etiquette that specifies the good behavior on the internet.

6. *a.* URL: Uniform Resource Locator

   b. SSH: Secure Shell

7. Shareware is not identical to the open source software or free software because:

   a. The user is not allowed to make modifications in it.

   b. The source code of the software is not available.

SECTION 'B' (15 Marks)

8. *a.* Two popular internet service providers in India are: Airtel and BSNL.

   b. Two websites that could help him search for the required information are google.com and yahoo.com.
   (Answer may vary)

9. SSL is a secure data transmission technology that transfers the data from the sender to the receiver over a secure network by encoding the original message. This encoding is known as encryption.

10. *a.* In HTML, there are five types of alignments available to align an image. These alignments are top, bottom, middle, left, and right.

    b. In the above code, the value center of the attribute align is invalid here.

If we want to center align an image, we need to use the `<CENTER>` tag, because the middle alignment cannot align an image at the center of a web page. Instead, it aligns the image in between of the text.

11. Refer to the following table:

Login Id element is	Text box
Classes element is	Radio button
Course Type element is	Dropdown box
Submit element is	Submit button
The form element for classes is	Radio button
The form element for course Type is	Dropdown box

OR

Post method

a. Appends form-data inside the body of the HTTP request (data is not shown in the URL).

b. Form submissions with POST cannot be bookmarked.

12. Anchor `<A>` tag is used to insert the link. HREF, that is, hyper reference is the mandatory attribute, which is used to link the specified document/image or a web page.

13. Refer to the following code:

```
<HTML>
<HEAD>
<TITLE> Image </TITLE>
</HEAD>
<BODY>
<CENTER><IMG SRC= “image.png” align = “center”>
</CENTER>
</BODY>
</HTML>
```

14. *a.* The <select> tag is used to create a dropdown box that prompts the user to select an item/item(s) from the list.

b. Multiple attribute of <select> tag allows multiple selections from the list.

OR

Refer to the following code:

```
<html>
```

```
<body>
<form method=”post”>
<INPUT TYPE=”radio” NAME=”orbits” VALUE=”strongly_agree”>Strongly
agree<BR>
<INPUT TYPE=”radio” NAME=”orbits” VALUE=”agree”>Agree<BR>
<INPUT TYPE=”radio” NAME=”orbits” VALUE=”no_opinion”>No opinion<BR>
<INPUT TYPE=”radio” NAME=”orbits” VALUE=”disagree”>Disagree<BR>
<INPUT TYPE=”radio” NAME=”orbits” VALUE=”strongly_disagree”>
Strongly disagree<BR>
</form>
</body>
</html>
```

SECTION 'C' (Scratch)

15. The move 10 steps block moves a sprite10 steps forward. You can change the number of steps by entering the new numeric value in the text field.

OR

The operators block is used to perform arithmetic, logical operations and various functions in a script. These are Light green in color, whereas the Sensing category includes blocks related to the recognition of different situations that occur on the stage concerning, sprites and the mouse among others, blocks to pull data from the keyboard, and blocks associated with the timer, date and camera. These are blue in color.

16. There are six types of block shapes are available in scratch. These are:

a. Hat blocks: These are the blocks that start every script. They are shaped with a roundedtop and a bump at the bottom.

b. Reporter blocks: Reporter blocks hold the values in the form of numbers and strings.

c. Stack blocks: These blocks perform the main commands. They are shaped with a notch at the top and a bump on the bottom.

d. Boolean blocks: These Blocks represent conditional statements. Their resultant value is either True or False, or Yes or No.

e. C blocks: Also known as wrap blocks, these blocks loop the blocks within the Cs or check if a condition is true.

f. Cap blocks: Cap blocks are the blocks that end the scripts. They are shaped with a notch at the top and a flat bottom.

17. To lengthen the game to 40 seconds, change both the values of x in the timing script to 40.

SECTION 'D' (Python)

18. The `range()` function is used to generate a series within a given range. It can take three parameters namely - start, stop and step value.

19. `aaaaaa`

20. *a.* 25

b. 450.0

21. Refer to the following code:

```
a=int(input("Enter the number : "))
f=1
i=1
while i<=a:
    f=f*i
    i=i+1

print("The factorial of ",a,"=",f)
```

Computer Application (CBSE) Code-165

Sample Question Paper 4

M.M. 30 **Time: 2 hrs**

General instructions

- **This paper contains 4 sections-Section A, Section B, Section C, and Section D.**
- **Section A and B has to be attempted by all students.**
- **Students may attempt any one of the two sections from Section C (Scratch) and Section D (Python).**

SECTION 'A' (7 Marks)

1. Write down one difference between a webpage and a website. **(1)**
2. What is the significance of using the <IMG> tag? **(1)**
3. How does accidental plagiarism occurs? **(1)**
4. What is the use of "To" in an e-mail message? **(1)**

   OR

   Name any two popular e-learning websites.
5. What is a DRM? **(1)**
6. What are the two protocols that are used for communication between computers? **(1)**
7. What are the benefits of e-commerce? **(1)**

SECTION 'B' (15 Marks)

8. The XYZ bank has started the facility of e-banking for its customers. Mention two benefits that the customers will get by using the service. **(2)**
9. Palvi and Muneesh are friends. Once while Palvi was buying some products online, somehow Muneesh stole her credentials. What kind of cyberattack was that? **(2)**

10. Name the following with respect to HTML: **(2)**

a. Defines the currently selected cell as table header.

b. Defines the title or caption of the table.

OR

Write down the names and description of the attributes of the Form tag.

11. How would you create a web page that will use a single-line text input used to take the Name and e-mail address of a user? **(2)**

12. Define the following terms: **(2)**

a. Cellpadding

b. Cellspacing

13. Observe the following picture and generate the code for it. **(2)**

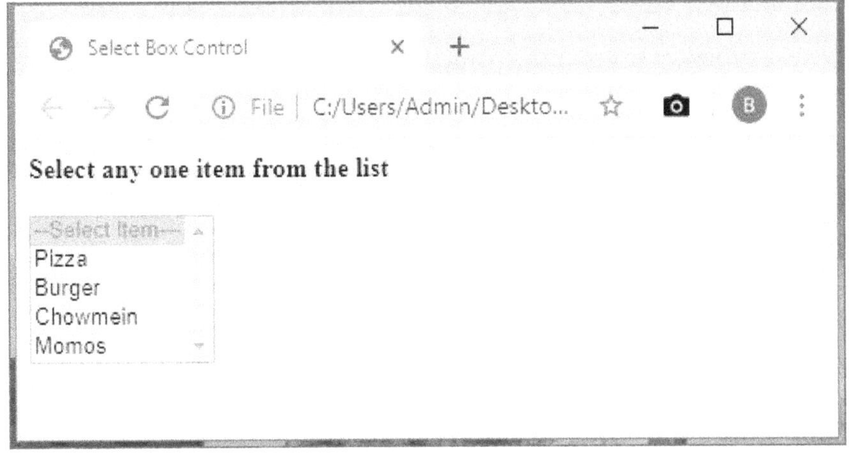

14. Explain the attributes of the <TD> and <TH> elements. **(3)**

OR

How to create a web page that will insert a video by using video tag.

SECTION 'C' (Scratch) (8 Marks)

15. What is the purpose of motion blocks? **(2)**

OR

What is the use of when space key pressed?

16. How to add the backdrop of the sprite to the stage? Write down the steps. **(4)**

17. How could you make the cat move slower? **(2)**

SECTION 'D' (Python) **(8 Marks)**

18. What is the difference between the while loop and the for loop? **(1)**

19. What will be the output of the following code? **(2)**

```
x = "abcdef"
i = "i"
    while i in x:
 print(i, end=" ")
```

20. Out of the following, find those identifiers, which cannot be used for naming variables and functions in a Python programming language: **(2)**

`Roll#No, continue, True, 41stno, _v1, No_2, false, Var1`

21. Write a program to enter the principal, rate, and interest, and calculate simple interest. **(3)**

Answers

SECTION 'A'

1. A web site is a collection of several web pages, whereas a web page is a single page that is formatted by using HTML language.
2. The `<IMG>` tag is used to insert images in a webpage.
3. Accidental plagiarism occurs when a person neglects to cite their sources, or misquotes their sources, or unintentionally paraphrases a source by using similar words, groups of words, and/or the sentence structure, without attribution.
4. "To" field is used to write the email address of the person to whom the message is to be sent. It asks the user to enter the recipient's email address.

   OR

   Some popular e-learning sites are Khan Academy and Coursera.
   (Answer may vary)
5. It is the solution that protects our software from being scraped for source codes, using de-compilers. It prevents our source code from being leaked.

6. The TCP and IP protocols are used for communication among computers.

7. The benefits of e-commerce include 24X7 availability, speed of delivering products, easy accessibility, and international reach.

SECTION 'B'

8. The two benefits that the customers will get by using the e-banking service are as follows:

a. A customer can perform banking transactions electronically without having to visit an actual bank.

b. The delivery of cash can be done instantly to customers by using the Automated Teller Machine (ATM).

9. A cyber-attack of this type is called phishing. When the person deliberately steals another person's username and password for some illegal purpose, or for his/her means, then it is a cybercrime and is known as phishing attack.

10. *a.* `<TH>`

b. `<CAPTION>`

OR

Attribute	Description
Action	This attribute specifies the URL where the form data is sent when the form is submitted. The URL is called the destination of the form.
Method	Specifies the HTTP method to be used when the form is submitted.
	a. Get: The form data issubmitted as URL variables.
	b. Post: The form data is submitted as an HTTP post.
Name	This attribute defines a unique name for the form, as there can be multiple forms on a web page. However, the form name will not be displayed on the form. The name attribute is optional if there is only one form on the web page.

11. Refer to the following code:

```
<html>
<head>
<title>Textbox control</title>
</head>
```

```
<body>
<form method="post">
Name: <INPUT type="text" name="firstname" size=20 maxlength=100 >
<BR><BR>
Email: <input name="text" type="text" name="email" size=20 max-
length=100 >
</form>
</body>
</html>
```

12. *a.* Cellpadding is used to set the amount of space between the contents of the cell and the cell wall.

    b. Cellspacing is used to set the space between the cells of a table.

13. Refer to the following code:

```
<html>
<head>
<title>Select Box Control</title>
</head>
<body>
<form>
<b>Select any one item from the list<b><br><br>
<select name="Item" size=5 multiple>
<option selected disabled>--Select Item---</option>
<option value="Pizza" >Pizza</option>
<option value="Burger" >Burger</option>
<option value="Chowmein" >Chowmein</option>
<option value="Momos" >Momos</option>
</select>
</form>
</body>
</html>
```

14. The attributes of the `<TD>` and `<TH>` elements are:

    a. Align attribute: Align attribute is similar to that of a table, except that it aligns the text inside the cell,rather than the table.

b. NoWrap attribute: The NoWrap attribute does not allow the text to flow to the next line in the cell. If the sentence is wider than the width of the cell, then NoWrap will show the sentence in one straight line.

c. COLSPAN attribute: The `Colspan` attribute helps in merging two or more columns of a table. This attribute is used with the `<TD>` or `<TH>` tag.

d. ROWSPAN attribute: The `Rowspan` attribute helps in merging two or more rows of a table. This attribute is used with the `<TD>` or `<TH>` tag.

OR

Refer to the following code:

```
<html>
<body>
<video width="320"height="240"controls>
<source src="sample-video.mp4"type="video/mp4">
<source src="sample-video.ogg"type="video/ogg">
<source src="sample-video.webm"type="video/webm">
</video>
</body>
</html>
```

SECTION 'C' (Scratch)

15. Motion blocks are used to control the movement, rotation, and position of the sprites on the stage.

OR

It starts the script when a specified key is pressed.

16. Follow the given steps to change the backdrop of the sprite:

1) Click on `Stage`.
2) Select `Choose Backdrop` from library.
3) A large set of backdrops show up. Choose any one and click on `OK` from the dialog box to add the backdrop to the stage.

17. To make the cat move slower, change the number in each of its three-move block to less than 10. For example, if we type in 5, the cat will move at half the speed.

SECTION 'D' (Python)

18. The `while` loop repeats a statement or a group of statements, while a given condition is TRUE. It tests the condition before executing the loop body.

    The for loop executes a sequence of statements multiple times and abbreviates the code that manages the loop variable.

19. No output.

20. Roll#No, Continue, True.

21. Refer to the following code:

```
p=float(input("Enter principal amount ; "))
r=float(input("Enter rate ; "))
t=float(input("Enter time : "))
simple=(p*r*t)/100
print("Simple Interest=", simple)
```

Computer Application (CBSE) Code-165

Sample Question Paper 5

M.M. 30 **Time: 2 hrs**

General instructions

- **This paper contains 4 sections-Section A, Section B, Section C, and Section D.**
- **Section A and B has to be attempted by all students.**
- **Students may attempt any one of the two sections from Section C (Scratch) and Section D (Python).**

SECTION 'A' (7 Marks)

1. What is e-reservation? **(1)**
2. Explain the function of the ALINK attribute used in HTML. **(1)**
3. Discuss the purpose of Kerberos. **(1)**
4. Expand the following acronyms: **(1)**
   a. SMTP
   b. POP3

   OR

   Write the web extensions for the following type of organizations.

   a. Education

   b. Government
5. What does plagiarism mean? **(1)**
6. Nishi is desperately interested in joining a weight loss program. But she has a lot of questions in her mind that she wants to discuss with people across the world. Name the tool that facilitates such social discussions. **(1)**
7. What are the functions of the Secure File Transfer Protocol? (*Any two*) **(1)**

SECTION 'B' (15 Marks)

8. Sidharth wants to improve his knowledge. He is using the search engine to gather the information. **(2)**

a. Define search engine.

b. Write down the examples of search engine. (*Any two*)

9. What are the ethical issues involved in e-commerce? **(2)**

10. Name the following with respect to HTML: **(2)**

a. Which tag is used to draw a horizontal line?

b. Which tag is used to create the heading?

OR

What is the difference between the `<SUP>` tag and the `<SUB>` tag?

11. Write the HTML code to produce a horizontal line of Aqua color. **(2)**

12. Observe the following HTML image and write down its code. **(2)**

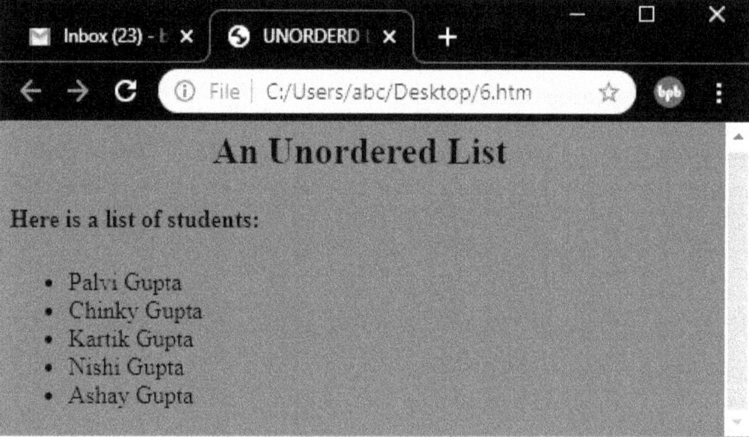

13. Name the following with respect to the `<audio>` tag: **(2)**

a. What is the use of an <audio> tag?

b. How can you insert audio in different file formats?

14. Write the HTML code to generate the form as shown in the below screenshot. **(3)**

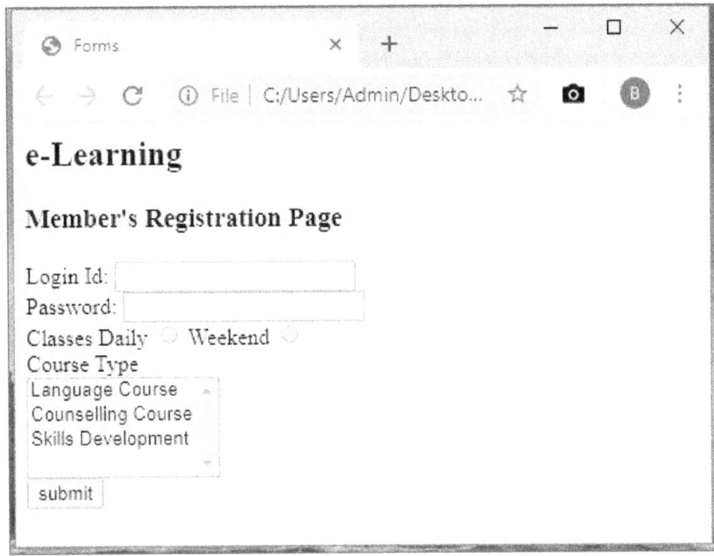

OR

Write the HTML code to display the following table specifications:

a. The title of the webpage is `Schedule.`

b. The caption of the table is `Duty Chart`.

c. `8 AM, 10 AM, 12 AM` are the headings given to the table.

SECTION 'C' (Scratch) **(8 Marks)**

15. What is the purpose of 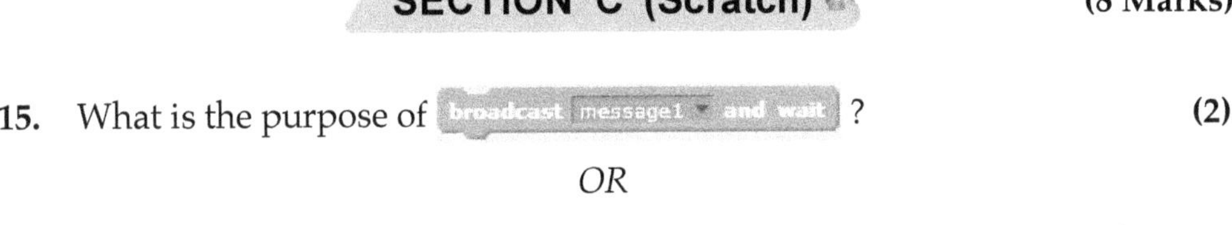

? **(2)**

OR

Write a program in scratch to input your name, age, and date of birth.

16. In how many ways you can add a backdrop in scratch? **(4)**

17. The following script should make the cat move across the stage slowly, but when I click the green flag to run it, nothing happens! What is wrong? **(2)**

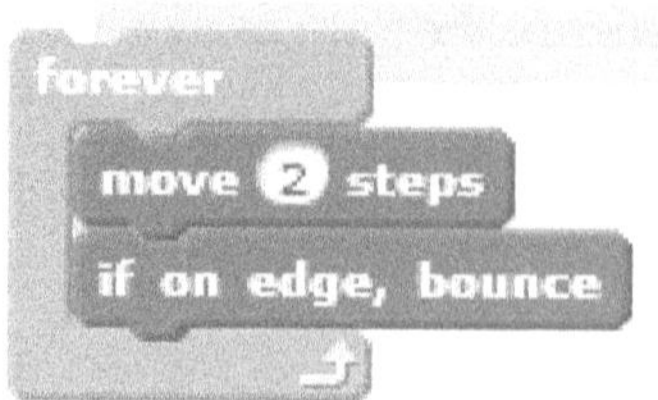

SECTION 'D' (Python) (8 Marks)

18. Define the conditional flow of statement. (1)

19. Find the output of the following code fragment. (2)

```
m=10
n=20
print(m+n)
```

20. How many times are the following loops executed? (2)

```
        i=100
while i<=200:
    print i
    i+=20
```

21. Write a program in Python to swap the values of two variables. (3)

Answers

SECTION 'A'

1. E-reservation is the process of reserving tickets online.
2. The `ALINK` attribute is used to change the color of the active link.
3. Kerberos is a third-party authentication that validates the clients over the network. It provides secure communication to network resources.
4. *a.* SMTP: Simple Mail Transfer Protocol

   b. POP: Post Office Protocol 3

   OR

   a. The `.edu` extension is for education.

   b. .gov is for government.

5. Plagiarism is the act of stealing others' creative ideas, thoughts, creation of art, music, and more, and marking them as our own.
6. Blog or weblog.
7. The functions of Secure File Transfer Protocol are as follows:
   a. It transmits files over the network in the most reliable way.
   b. It provides security of data while transmitting from one system to another system.

SECTION 'B'

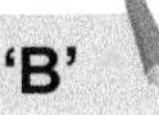

8. *a.* A search engine searches for information on the internet and displays it on our computer screen.
   b. Google and Bing are the examples of search engines.
9. The ethical issues in e-commerce are as follows:
   a. E-commerce consumer privacy: Sensitive information such as debit or credit card CVC numbers and other details must be protected from intruders. Private information should be adequate and not be kept for longer than the necessary time.
   b. E-commerce security: It refers to the security of data that should be accessible only to authorized users, in a safe and reliable manner. It makes sure that the data is collected accurately and reliably.
   c. E-commerce trust: It is also known as e-trust. It refers that the product which is purchased online is exactly the same as what has been ordered by the consumer.
10. *a.* `<HR>`
    b. `<H1>`

OR

The `<SUP>` tag is used to create a superscript in a web page, in which the selected text is placed slightly above the line of the regular text, whereas the `<SUB>` tag is used to create a subscript on a web page, in which the selected text is placed slightly below the line of the regular text.

11. Refer to the following code:

```
<HTML>
<HEAD>
```

```
<TITLE> Horizontal Line </TITLE>
</HEAD>
<BODY><HR COLOR = "Aqua" ></BODY>
</HTML>
```

12. Refer to the following code:

```
<HTML>
<HEAD>
<TITLE> UNORDERED LIST </TITLE>
</HEAD>
<BODY BGCOLOR = "Red">
<H2 ALIGN = "CENTER"> An Unorderd List </H2>
<H4> Here is a list of students:</H4>
<UL>
<LI> Palvi Gupta</LI>
<LI> Chinky Gupta</LI>
<LI> Kartik Gupta</LI>
<LI> Nishi Gupta</LI>
<LI> Ashay Gupta</LI>
<UL>
</BODY>
</HTML>
```

13. *a.* The audio tag is used to add sound and music in the HTML page. It is used in conjunction with thesource tag.

b. Refer to the following code:

```
<html>
<body>
<audio controls>
<source src="sample.ogg" type="audio/ogg">
<source src="kalimba.mp3" type="audio/mpeg">
<source src="jazz.wav" type="audio/wav">
</audio>
</body>
</html>
```

14. Refer to the following code:

```
<html>
<head><title>Forms</title></head>
<body>
<h2>e-Learning</h2>
<h3>Member's Registration Page</h3>
<form method="post" action="Forms.html">
Login Id: <input type="text" name="id"><br>
Password: <input type="password" name="pswd"><br>
Classes Daily <input type="radio" name="classes" value="Daily">
Weekend <input type="radio" name="classes" value="Weekend">
<br>
Course Type<br>
<select name="cType" multiple>
<option value="Language Course">Language Course</option>
<option value="Counselling Course">CounsellingCourse</option>
<option value="Skills Development">SkillsDevelopment</option>
</select>
<br>
<input type="Submit" value="Submit">
</form>
</body>
</html>
```

OR

Refer to the following code:

```
<HTML>
<HEAD>
<TITLE>Schedule</TITLE>
</HEAD>
<BODY>
<TABLE Border = 1>
<CAPTION>Duty Chart</CAPTION>
<TR>
```

```
<TH> 8 A.M </TH>
<TH> 10 A.M </TH>
<TH> 12 A.M </TH>
</TR>
<TR>
<TD> Palvi </TD>
<TD> Ankita </TD>
<TD> Swati </TD>
</TR>
</TABLE>
</BODY>
</HTML>
```

SECTION 'C' (Scratch)

15. This block is used for sending the specified broadcast by the script and letting them wait till all the scripts by the broadcast are activated. This is mainly used to pass messages between sprites.

OR

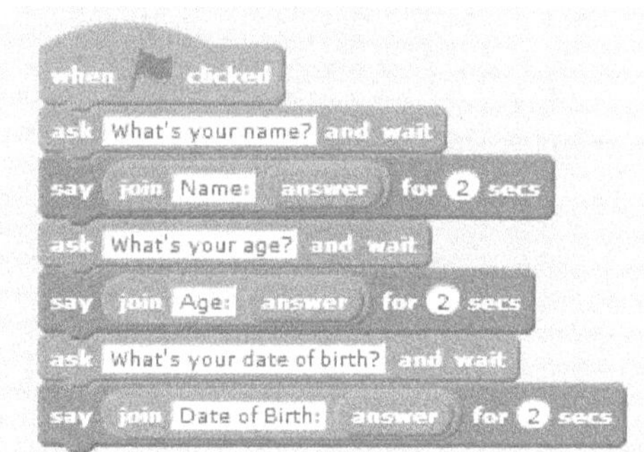

16. There are three ways to add a backdrop in scratch. They are:

a. Paint new backdrop: Click on the Paint new backdrop button to open the Paint Editor in scratch, where we can draw a new backdrop.

b. Upload backdrop from file: Click on the `Upload backdrop` from file button to transfer an image file from your computer to our project.

c. New backdrop from Camera: Click on the `New backdrop` from Camera button to use our webcam to snap a picture that can be used as backdrop in our project.

17. In this script, the when [flag] clicked (when green flag clicked) block is missing. You need the when [flag] clicked block on top.

SECTION 'D' (Python)

18. When a program consists of one, or more than one condition, on which the execution of the statements depends, it is known as a conditional flow of statement.

19. 30.

20. 6 times.

21. Refer to the following code:

```
a=int(input("Enter first number : "))
b=int(input("Enter second number : "))
print("The values of a and b before swapping are: ", a,b)
temp=a
a=b
b=temp
print("The values of a and b after swapping are: ", a,b)
```

Revise forms in HTML and Inserting Multimedia

Go to: https://qrgo.page.link/2ntoZ Or Scan:

Computer Application (CBSE) Code-165

Sample Question Paper 6

M.M. 30 **Time: 2 hrs**

General instructions

- **This paper contains 4 sections-Section A, Section B, Section C, and Section D.**
- **Section A and B has to be attempted by all students.**
- **Students may attempt any one of the two sections from Section C (Scratch) and Section D (Python).**

SECTION 'A' (7 Marks)

1. What is the use of HTTPs? **(1)**
2. Name the attribute that is used for aligning an image in HTML? **(1)**
3. What is the meaning of Digital Property Rights? **(1)**
4. What is the main objective of a network? **(1)**

   OR

   Write down one advantage of e-reservation.
5. How does mosaic plagiarism occur? **(1)**
6. How is a web client is related to HTTP? **(1)**
7. Give one example of plagiarism. **(1)**

SECTION 'B' (15 Marks)

8. Explain 4G technology and its four features. **(2)**
9. Which mechanism prevents eavesdropping? Explain. **(2)**
10. Name the following with respect to the `<Body>` tag: **(2)**

    a. Purpose of the <Body> tag.

    b. Attributes of the <Body> tag.

11. Write the HTML code to create a paragraph whose text color is Yellow. **(2)**

OR

What happens when the"submit" or "reset" buttons get activated?

12. Name the following with respect to the `<embed>` tag: **(2)**

    a. Write down the syntax for inserting a video using the `<embed>` tag.

    b. Name and describe the attributes used with the embed tag.

13. Write the HTML code for the following: **(2)**

    a. H_2O

    b. $X_2 + Y_2$

14. Observe the following picture and generate the code for it: **(3)**

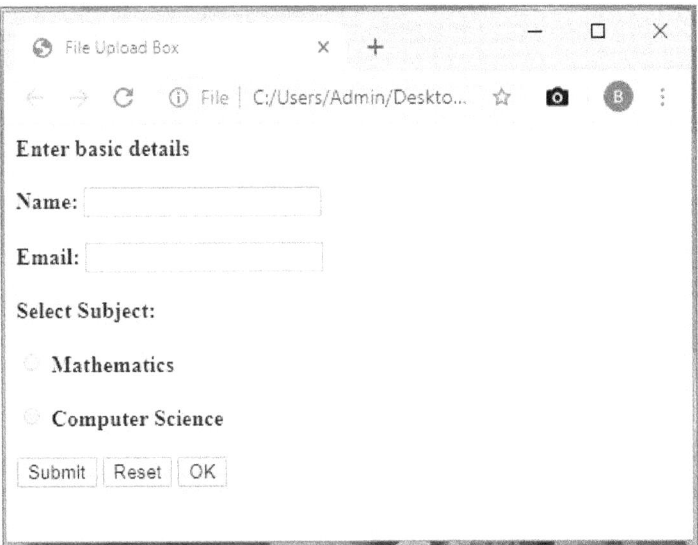

OR

Create the following table in HTML by using suitable tags:

The Student Details Record					
Student Roll No	Student Name	Marks			Total Marks
		English	Maths	Science	
101	Muneesh	20	18	40	78
102	Sidharth	19	20	18	57
103	Nishi	19	19	17	55
104	Kartik	18	17	30	65

SECTION 'C' (Scratch) (8 Marks)

15. What is the purpose of the operator block in scratch? **(2)**

OR

What is the purpose of the if block in scratch?

16. Explain five motion blocks? **(4)**

17. Test your scratch script reading powers! What does this script do? Read it carefully and try to act out each block in your mind **(2)**

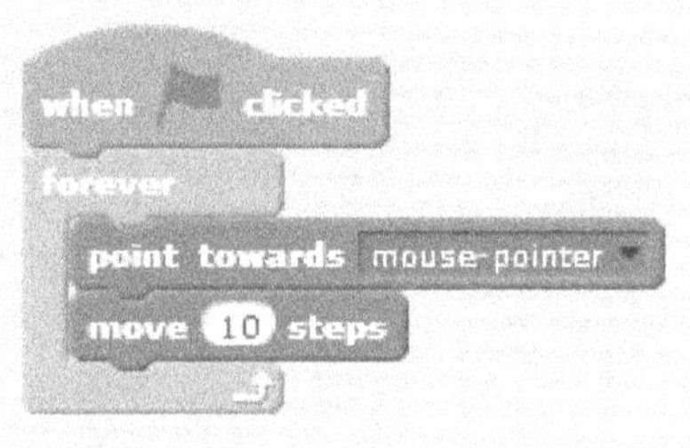

SECTION 'D' (Python) (8 Marks)

18. What is a keyword? How many keywords are available in python? **(2)**

19. What are punctuators and what are the different types of punctuators? **(2)**

20. What will be the output of following code: **(2)**

```
print("take every change.")
print("drop every fear.")
```

21. Write a program to take the values of length and breadth of a rectangle from the user and check if it is square or not. **(2)**

Answers

SECTION 'A'

1. HTTPs is used to protect highly confidential online transactions, like online banking and online shopping order forms.
2. The ALIGN attribute is used to align an image in HTML.
3. A digital property is the property that is created online or digitally. This property may be our own creation, picture, art, music, video clips, and more.
4. The main objective of the network is to share the data or information among several users.

OR

It provides global access to the customers for booking from anywhere at any time.

5. Mosaic plagiarism occurs when a student borrows phrases from a source without using quotation marks or finds synonyms for the author's language while retaining the same general structure and the meaning of the original.
6. A web client is an application (web browser) that communicates with a web server, using Hypertext Transfer Protocol (HTTP).
7. Suppose that a college lecturer has written an article on some topic, but some other person publishes that article under his own name or in an unauthorized way, this is known as plagiarism.

SECTION 'B'

8. 4G mobile technology uses ultra-high broadband internet services, with much faster and higher data speed, typically between 100 MBps-1 GBps.

The features of 4G Technology are as follows:

a. It is used for internet access on computers and it will be totally wireless.

b. 4G provides internet access, high quality video streaming and anytime, anywhere voice and data transmission, at a much faster speed than 3G.

c. Delivering faster and better mobile broadband experiences.

- Providing more data capacity, for richer content and more connections.

9. Data encryption mechanism prevents eavesdropping. Data encryption is the method of securing the data when it is sent over the network. The original data is first encrypted and then transferred from the sender'send. When it reaches to the receiver, the data is decrypted or decoded so as to get the original message.

10. *a.* The <Body> tag contains all the tags and information that we want to view in a web page.

    b. The attributes of the <Body> tag are, BACKGROUND, BGCOLOR, TEXT, LINK, LEFTMARGIN, and TOPMARGIN.

11. Refer to the following code:

```
<HTML>
<HEAD>
<TITLE> PARAGRAPH </TITLE>
</HEAD>
<BODY>
<P><FONT COLOR= "Yellow"> My name is Sidharth. I love my family.
</FONT></P>
</BODY>
</HTML>
```

OR

A submit button, when activated, submits a form. A form may contain more than one submit button. The reset button, when activated, resets all the controls to their initial values.

12. *a.* The syntax for inserting a video using the <embed> tag:

```
<embed src="URL of the video"autostart="false/true
"height="value"width="value" />
```

    b. Refer to the following table:

Attribute	Description
Src	It provides the URL of the video to be inserted.
Height	Height of the video.
Width	Width of the video.
Autostart	Value may be false or true.

13. Refer to the following code:

```
<HTML>

<HEAD>

<TITLE> Subscript</TITLE>

</HAED>

<BODY>

The chemical formula of water is H<SUB>2</SUB>O.

</BODY>

</HTML>
```

b. Refer to the following code:

```
<HTML>

<HEAD>

<TITLE> Superscript</TITLE>

</HAED>

<BODY>

The equation is X<SUP>2</SUP> + Y<SUP>2</SUP>.

</BODY>

</HTML>
```

14. Refer to the following code:

```
<html>

<head>

<title>File Upload Box</title>

</head>

<body>

<form>

<b> Enter basic details</><br><br>

Name: <INPUT type="text" name="firstname" size=20 maxlength=100 >

<BR><BR>

Email: <input name="text" type="text" name="email" size=20 max-
length=100 >

<br><br>

<b>Select Subject:</b><BR><BR>
```

```
<input type="radio"name="subject" value="maths"> Mathematics <BR>
<BR>
<input type="radio"name="subject" value="cs"> Computer Science
<br><br>
<input type="submit"name="submit"value="Submit">
<input type="reset"name="reset"value="Reset">
<input type="button"name="ok"value="OK">
</form>
</body>
</html>
```

OR

Refer to the following code:

```
<HTML>
<HEAD>
<TITLE></TITLE>
</HEAD>
<BODY>
<TABLE BORDER="1">
<TR>
<TH COLSPAN=6 ALIGN="center"> The Student Details Record</TH>
</TR>
<TR>
<TH ROWSPAN=2>Student Roll No</TH>
<TH ROWSPAN=2> Student Name</TH>
<TH COLSPAN=3> Marks </TH>
<TH ROWSPAN=2>Total Marks</TH>
</TR>
<TR>
<TH>English</TH>
<TH>Maths</TH>
<TH>Science</TH>
</TR>
<TR>
```

```
<TD>100 </TD>
<TD> Munesh</TD>
<TD> 20 </TD>
<TD> 18 </TD>
<TD> 40 </TD>
<TD> 78 </TD>
</TR>
<TR>
<TD>101 </TD>
<TD> Sidharth </TD>
<TD> 19 </TD>
<TD> 20 </TD>
<TD> 18 </TD>
<TD> 57 </TD>
</TR>
<TR>
<TD>102 </TD>
<TD> Nishi </TD>
<TD> 19 </TD>
<TD> 19 </TD>
<TD> 17 </TD>
<TD> 55 </TD>
</TR>
<TR>
<TD>103 </TD>
<TD> Kartik </TD>
<TD> 18 </TD>
<TD> 17 </TD>
<TD> 30</TD>
<TD> 65 </TD>
</TR>
</TABLE>
</BODY>
</HTML>
```

SECTION 'C' (Scratch)

15. The operators block is used to perform arithmetic and logical operations, and various functions in a script. These are light green in color.

OR

The if block allows you to execute statements only when certain conditions are met.

16. Motion blocks control the movement of sprites. These are medium blue in color. There are 17 motion blocks, 14 stack blocks and 3 reporter blocks. It changes the angle of the movement of the sprite according to the X-axis and theY-axis.

The commands of the motion block are as follows:

a. go to mouse-pointer : To follow where the mouse cursor is, or go to a random position.

b. change x by 10 : To move left or right by a number of steps.

c. change y by 10 : To move up or down by a number of steps.

d. go to x: 0 y: 0 : To go to any position, x is between -240 and 240, y between -180 and 180.

e. x position : The value of the x position, where the sprite is currently is.

17. The script makes the cat run towards the mouse pointer on the stage.

SECTION 'D' (Python)

18. Keywords are the reserved words that cannot be used for creating variables, functions, classes or any other identifiers. Keywords are case sensitive, which means that there is a difference between the lowercase and uppercase keywords. There are 33 keywords available in python.

19. Punctuators are the symbols that are used to organize the sentence structures. The various types of punctuators are:

a. ' (Single Quote)

b. " (Double Quote)

c. # (Hash)

d. \ (forward slash)

e. ( ) (parenthesis)

f. [ ] (Square bracket)

g) { } (Curly bracket)

h) @ (at the rate)

i) , (comma)

j) : (colon)

k) . (dot)

l) = (Assignment)

20. take every change.
drop every fear.

21. Refer to the following code:

```
print ("Enter length")
length = input()
print ("Enter breadth")
breadth = input()
if length == breadth
  print ("Yes, it is square")
else:
print ("No, it is only Rectangle")
```

Computer Application (CBSE) Code-165

Sample Question Paper 7

M.M. 30 **Time: 2 hrs**

General instructions

- **This paper contains 4 sections-Section A, Section B, Section C, and Section D.**
- **Section A and B has to be attempted by all students.**
- **Students may attempt any one of the two sections from Section C (Scratch) and Section D (Python).**

SECTION 'A' (7 Marks)

1. Write down one function of SFTP. **(1)**
2. What are the different methods of using style sheets? **(1)**
3. Explain the purpose of the Open Source License. **(1)**
4. Write down any two sites that will help you find people on the internet. **(1)**

   OR

   Write down one function of the SMTP protocol.
5. What is the meaning of Intellectual Property Rights? **(1)**
6. Define hacking. **(1)**
7. Write down the advantages of E-reservation. *(Any two)* **(1)**

SECTION 'B' (15 Marks)

8. What is a modem? Explain how it works. What are its two types? **(2)**
9. Explain the different types of Digital Responsibilities. **(2)**
10. Write down the following with respect to HTML: **(2)**

    a. Name the tag that is used for the ordered list.

b. Name the tag that is used for the unordered list.

11. Observe the following screenshot and write down its HTML code: **(2)**

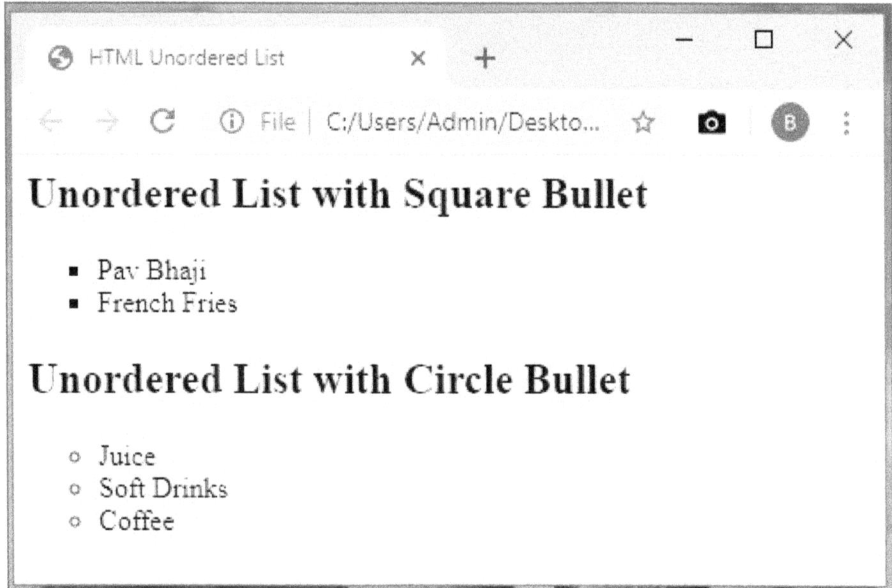

12. Write the HTML code to create a web page that will insert an image. **(2)**

OR

Differentiate between the radio button and the checkbox control.

13. Observe the following screenshot and write down its code. **(2)**

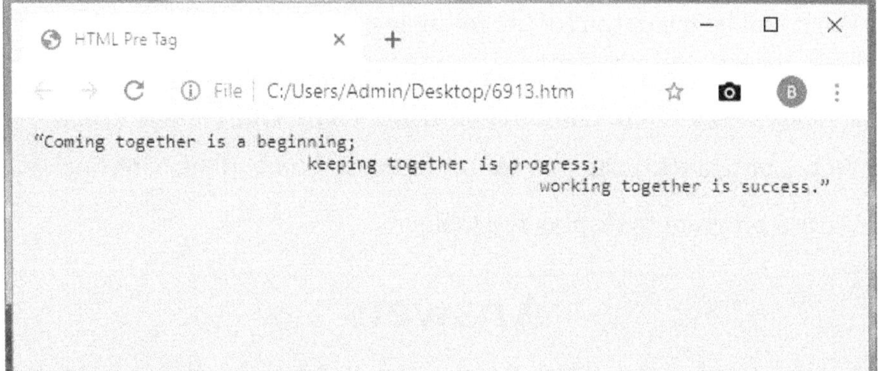

14. How to create a web page using the title attribute as Alink. **(3)**

OR

Observe the following screenshot and write down its code.

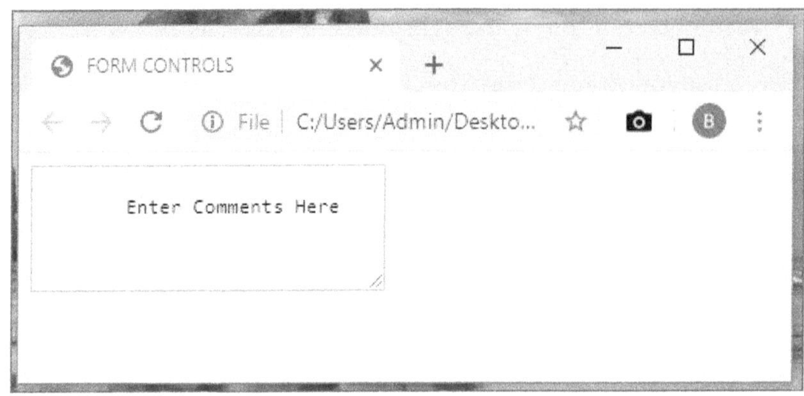

SECTION 'C' (Scratch) (8 Marks)

15. What is the use of sound block? **(2)**

OR

Explain the meaning of the hat and reporter blocks.

16. Explain the motion block and its functions. *(Any nine)* **(4)**

17. How to create a variable using the data block in scratch? **(2)**

SECTION 'D' (Python) (8 Marks)

18. Explain there lational operators and their types. **(2)**

19. What will be the output of the following code? **(2)**

```
num1, num2, num3=7,6,5
print(num1, num2, num3)
```

20. Write a program to enter the number of feet and convert them into inches. **(2)**

21. Write a program to display the table of 2. **(2)**

Answers

SECTION 'A'

1. SFTP provides the security of data while transmitting it from one system to another system.

2. There are three ways you can apply CSS to an HTML document - *in-line, Internal* and *External*.

3. Open source license allows the user to modify and share the software with other users, without seeking permission from the company or the organization.

4. The sites that help you find people on the internet are: http://www.people.yahoo.com and http://www.classmates.com. (Answer may vary)

OR

It is the protocol and its function is to send e-mail messages to the recipient of messages.

5. Intellectual property rights refer to the right given by the owner of the property, pertaining to how much information should be exchanged, shared, or distributed.

6. Hacking is identifying the weakness in computer systems or networks, to exploit its weaknesses to gain access.

7. The advantages of e-reservation are as follows:

   a. We can check the availability of the seats by sitting at home.

   b. It provides global access to the customers for booking from anywhere at any time.

SECTION 'B'

8. The full form of Modem is Modulation and Demodulation. It is a computer peripheral device that allows us to connect and communicate with other computers via telephone lines. It converts the digital data into analog data, and vice-versa. The process of converting the digital data into analog data is called Modulation and the process of converting analog data into digital data is called Demodulation.

   There are two type of Modem:

   a. Internal Modem: Internal Modem is a Modem that is placed inside the CPU. It is in the form of a card.

   b. External Modem: External Modem is a Modem that is placed outside the CPU. It is a box-shaped device.

9. The various digital responsibilities are:

   a. Reportany kind of bullying, harassing or identity theft.

b. Cite works used for resources and researching.

c. Download music, videos, and other material legally.

d. Model and teach student expectations of technology use.

e. Keep data/information safe from hackers.

f. Not to falsify our identity in any way.

g. Do not share any other person's personal information without permission.

h. Follow the rules and/or codes of conduct for every Internet site.

i. Respect the opinions and ideas of others.

j. Obey all intellectual property laws.

10. *a.* <OL>

b. <UL>

11. Refer to the following code:

```
<HTML>
<HEAD>
<TITLE>HTML font Tag</TITLE>
</HEAD>
<BODY>
<h2>Unordered List with Square Bullet</h2>
<ul type=”square”>
<li>Pav Bhaji</li>
<li>French Fries</li>
</ul>

<h2>Unordered List with Circle Bullet</h2>
<ul type=”circle”>
<li>Juice</li>
<li>Soft Drinks</li>
</ul>
</BODY>
</HTML>
```

12. Refer to the following code:

```
<HTML>
<head>
<title>Inserting Images</title>
</head>
<body>
    Trees are necessary for life.
<br>
<IMG src="trees.jpg" alt="Trees give life" height="150"
width="150" border="5">
</body>
</HTML>
```

OR

The radio button enables the selection of one of the options out of the many. Radio buttons operate as a groupand provide mutually exclusive selection values.

As compared to the radio button, a checkbox allows multiple selections of items. Each checkbox operates individually, so a user can toggle each response ON and OFF.

13. Refer to the following code:

```
<HTML>
<HEAD>
<TITLE>HTML Paragraph Tag</TITLE>
</HEAD>

<BODY bgcolor="pink" text="black">
<PRE>"Coming together is a beginning; keeping together is prog-
ress; working together is success."</PRE>
</BODY>
</HTML>
```

14. Refer to the following code:

```
<HTML>
<head>
<title> Inserting Links in HTML</title>
</head>
```

```
<body>
<A HREF="picture.HTML" Title="Hyperlink Created to know the de-
scription">Click here </A>
</body>
</HTML>
```

OR

Refer to the following code:

```
<HTML>
<HEAD>
<TITLE> FORM CONTROLS</TITLE>
</HEAD>
<BODY>
<form method="post" action="mailto:youremail@gmail.com">
<textarea rows="5" cols="30" wrap="physical" name="comments">
Enter Comments Here
</textarea>
</form>
</BODY>
</HTML>
```

SECTION 'C' (Scratch)

15. The sound block provides different blocks to add music to the scratch project. It also provides music based on different instruments using the set instrument to 1 block.

OR

Hat blocks: These are the blocks that start every script. They are shaped with a rounded top and a bump at the bottom.

Reporter blocks: Reporter blocks hold the values in the form of numbers and strings.

16. Motion blocks deal with the movement of sprites. The position of a sprite can be changed by changing the coordinates of X and Y. Motion blocks appear in dark blue color.

The Stage does not contain any Motion blocks since it is a still object.

BLOCK	FUNCTION
move (10) steps	Moves the sprite forward or backward the number of steps in the direction the sprite is facing.
turn ↻ (15) degrees	Turns the sprite (clockwise) by the specified amount.
turn ↺ (15) degrees	Turns the sprite (counter-clockwise) by the specified amount.
point in direction (90▾)	Points the sprite in the specified direction.
go to x: (0) y: (0)	Moves the sprite to the specified X and Y position.
change x by (10)	Changes the sprite's X position by the specified amount.
set x to (0)	Sets the sprite's X position to the specified amount.
change y by (10)	Changes the sprite's Y position by the specified amount.
set y to (0)	Sets the sprite's Y position to the specified amount.

17. In scratch, Variables are created by using a data block.

The various steps for creating a variable are:

a. Go to the blocks palette and click on the data category.

b. Click on `make a variable`. A dialog box will appear.

c. Type the name of the variable. It will show you two options.

i. For all sprites, that let we make a global variable.

ii. For this sprite only, that will let we make a local variable.

SECTION 'D' (Python)

18. These operators are also known as comparison operators because they compare two values and return the Boolean value as True or False.

Type of relational operators:

Operator	Description	Example
= =	If the values of the two operands are equal, then the condition becomes true.	(a == b) is not true.
!=	If the values of the two operands are not equal, then the condition becomes true.	(a!= b) is true.
>	If the value of the left operand is greater than the value of the right operand, then the condition becomes true.	(a > b) is not true.
<	If the value of the left operand is less than the value of the right operand, then the condition becomes true.	(a < b) is true.
>=	If the value of the left operand is greater than or equal to the value of the right operand, then the condition becomes true.	(a >= b) is not true.
<=	If the value of left operand is less than or equal to the value of the right operand, then the condition becomes true.	(a <= b) is true.

19. `7 6 5`

20. Refer to the following code:

```
feet=int(input("Enter number of feet : "))
inches=feet*12
print("Total number of inches are : ",inches)
```

21. Refer to the following code:

```
for num in range(1,11,1):
    print(2,"X",num,"=",num)
    print("\n")
```

Go to: https://qrgo.page.link/w2xPq Or Scan:

Computer Application (CBSE) Code-165

Sample Question Paper 8

M.M. 30 **Time: 2 hrs**

General instructions

- **This paper contains 4 sections-Section A, Section B, Section C, and Section D.**
- **Section A and B has to be attempted by all students.**
- **Students may attempt any one of the two sections from Section C (Scratch) and Section D (Python).**

SECTION 'A' (7 Marks)

1. Write down one advantage of Home page. **(1)**
2. Differentiate between the `ROWSPAN` and `COLSPAN` attributes? **(1)**
3. What does DRM mean? **(1)**
4. Write down one difference between 3G and 4G. **(1)**

OR

Name some of the popular ISP companies in India.

5. Who are hackers? **(1)**
6. List the different types of blogs. **(1)**
7. Define privacy. **(1)**

SECTION 'B' (15 Marks)

8. As life gets busier, it becomes difficult for everyone to keep a track with school and college friends, old colleagues, old neighbors and favorite teachers. It is important to keep in touch with all your near and dear ones. At times, people sitting miles away, doing similar activity or solving similar problems can help you achieve goals faster by sharing their experiences. Similarly, people belonging to different socio-economic backgrounds can change your perspective and can enhance your understanding of various cultures. **(2)**

a. Suggest two real-time tools that are suitable for the above-mentioned activities.

b. What is the generic name used for such tools?

9. Write about the various digital property rights. **(2)**

10. Name the following with respect with linking: **(2)**

a. What is the use of linking?

b. Name the attribute that is mandatory for linking.

OR

Write down the syntax and attributes of the textbox control.

11. In reference with the below CSS code, explain the usage of the background-repeat property. Also mention the different values that can be used for background-repeat. **(2)**

```
Body { background-image: url("learn.gif"); background-repeat: repeat-x}
```

12. What is the significance of using the font family property of FONTS? **(2)**

13. Write the following with respect to HTML: **(2)**

a. Which attribute sets the font color of the text on the web page?

b. Which attribute sets the color of the links on the web pages?

14. Observe the following code carefully and answer the questions that follow: **(3)**

```
<html>
<head>
<title>NETWORK SECURITY</title>
<style type="text/css">
li {
letter-spacing:10px ;
text-transform: lowercase;
}
</style>
</head>
<body> The Dos and Don't s of network security
<ol>
<li> KEEP ANTI-VIRUS SOFTWARE UP TO DATE.</li>
<li> SAVE THE FILE TO COMPUTER OR A DISK.</li>
```

```
<li> RUN AN ANTI-VIRUS SCAN REGULARLY.</li>
</ol>
</body>
</html>
```

Predict the output of the above code, while explaining the effects applied on `<li>` in the CSS code.

OR

How to create a web page that will show the vertical alignment of a text while the rows are merged?

SECTION 'C' (Scratch) (8 Marks)

15. What is the purpose of using the wait instruction and which block is used for this? **(2)**

OR

What is the significance of ask and answer?

16. Summarize the various blocks with their functioning. **(4)**

17. Suppose Palvi wants to move a sprite in a way that will draw a triangle. But, she does not know the steps to create the triangle. Help her in writing the script for the same. **(2)**

SECTION 'D' (Python) (8 Marks)

18. What are operators and operands? Explain with example. **(2)**

19. Rewrite the given code snippet using for loop **(2)**

```
sum=0
while i<10:
sum=sum+i
i=i+1
print("sum=",sum)
```

20. Write a program in Python to find the volume of a sphere. **(2)**

21. What is a string? How can you find the length of a string? **(2)**

Answers

SECTION 'A'

1. Home page helps the users to click on different links and get on to the required page.
2. The ROWSPAN attribute is used to merge (combine) two or more rows of a table. On the other hand, the COLSPAN attribute is used to merge two or more columns of a table.
3. DRM is Digital Rights Management (DRM). It is the digital property solution that protects the software from being scraped for source codes, using de-compilers. It prevents your source code from being leaked.
4. The speed of 4G is about 10 times faster than 3G. We can stream audio and video content using 4G.

   OR

   Some of the popular ISP companies in India are: MTNL, Airtel, Reliance, and BSNL.
5. Hackers are people with skills, who use their knowledge to gain unauthorized access to data in a system or a computer.
6. Some of the commonly used blogs are as follows:
   a. Personal blogs
   b. Corporate and organizational blogs
   c. Genre blogs
7. Privacy refers to controlling the dissemination and the use of data.

SECTION 'B'

8. *a.* Facebook and Twitter
   b. Social Networking
9. The different types of digital property rights are:
   a. Internet access for all
   b. Freedom of expression and association
   c. Access to knowledge

d. Shared learning and creation – free and open-source software and technology development

e. Privacy and data protection

f. Awareness, protection, and realization of rights

g. Network Equality

h. Right to freedom of expression

i. Right to report anyone or anything that seems inappropriate

10. *a.* Linking enables connection of several web pages to with each other.

b. `HREF`, that is, hyper reference, is the mandatory attribute that is used to link the specified document/image or a web page.

OR

Syntax of using textbox control:

```
<INPUT type=”text” name=”value” value=”initial value” size=”width
in number” maxlength=”length in numbers>
```

Attributes of textbox control: Refer to the following table:

Attributes used by input element for textbox control	Description
`type`	Indicates the type of input control, and for text input control, it will be set to text.
`name`	Used to give a name to the control, which is sent to the server to be recognized and get the value.
`value`	This can be used to provide an initial value inside the control.
`size`	Allows to specify the width of the text-input control in terms of characters.
`maxlength`	Allows to specify the maximum number of characters a user can enter into the text box.

11. With reference to the above CSS code, the inserted background image - `learn.gif`- will repeat horizontally on the browser screen.The four different values for `background-repeat` are as follows:

Value	Description
`background-repeat: repeat-x:`	The image is repeated horizontally.
`background-repeat: repeat-y:`	The image is repeated vertically.

`background-repeat: repeat:`	The image is repeated both horizontally and vertically.
`background-repeat: no-repeat:`	The image is not repeated.

12. The font-family property is used to apply a prioritized list of fonts on a web page. If the first font of the list is not installed on the computer, then the next font of the list will be displayed until a suitable font is found.

13. *a.* Text

    b. LINK

14. The output of the above code will be:

```
The Dos and Don’ts of network security
KEEP ANTI-VIRUS SOFTWARE UP TO DATE.
SAVE THE FILE TO COMPUTER OR A DISK.
RUN AN ANTI-VIRUS SCAN REGULARLY.
```

As per the output, it is evident that the list elements specified as `li` have been displayed in lower case due to: `text-transform: lowercase;`. Also, there is a space of `10` pixels between each letter due to: `letter-spacing:10px;`.

OR

Refer to the following code:

```
<HTML>
<head>
<title>Valign Attribute </title>
</head>
<body>
<table border=”2” bgcolor= “Pink” width=”30%” height=”30%”>
<tr>
<th colspan=”3>” Employee Details</th>
</tr>
<tr>
<td>Employee code </td>
<td>Basic Salary</td>
<td> Country</td>
</tr>
<tr>
```

```
<td>EM001</td>
<td>10000</td>
<td rowspan="2" valign="bottom">India</td>
</tr>
<tr>
<td>EM002</td>
<td>10500</td>
</tr>
</table>
</body>
</HTML>
```

SECTION 'C' (Scratch)

15. The `WAIT` instruction is needed to slow down the acting, so that we can see or hear it properly. We can get the wait instruction from the `CONTROL` menu.

OR

Ask and Wait prompts the users to type the input using the keyboard. The answer stores the keyboard input.

16. Refer to the following table:

Block	Description
Motion	This block is used to move, turn, set the position and define the motion of the sprite, including what to do when it touches the edge.
Looks	This block is used to make the sprite say, think, show, hide, switch costume/backdrop,and change color.
Sound	This block is used to play different sounds, stop, change the volume and tempo.
Pen	This block sets the pen size, color and makes the pen move up, down, and clear.
Events	We can make a block of code when a particular event occurs. Here are a few examples for events:
	a. a particular key is pressed,
	b. The mouse is pressed on an object
	c. make a loud noise!
Control	Control structures like `if…then`, `if…then…else`, `wait`, repeat loops, `if…then`, and `if…then…else` add intelligence to the program!

Sensing	It helps in sensing the situations of sensing (example, mouse down) and other environmental actions.
Operators	It helps in using various arithmetic and logical operators, random number generators and few functions.
Data	Create new variables (re-used in other scripts) and lists.

17. She should write the following script for drawing a triangle.

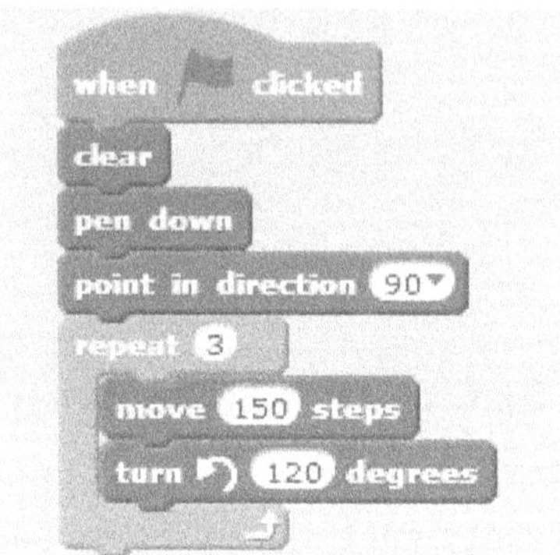

To draw a triangle,

a. Pen must be in drawing position.

b. Point in Right direction.

c. Repeat following commands 3 times:

  i. Move 150 steps.

  ii. Turn 120 degrees.

SECTION 'D' (Python)

18. Operators are used for performing various operations on values. For example, addition, subtraction, multiplication and division, and more.

Operands are the values or variables on which the operators work.

For example:

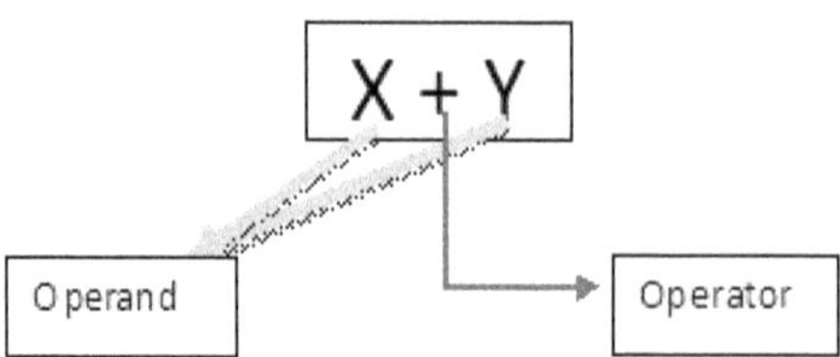

Here, X and Y are operands and + is an operator, which adds the values stored in X and Y.

19. Refer to the following code:

```
sum=0

i=0

for i in range(0,10,1):

sum=sum+i

print("sum=",sum)
```

20. Refer to the following code:

```
r=float(input("Enter radius : "))

pi = 3.14

r= 6.0

V= (4.0/3.0)*pi* (r**3)

print('The volume of the sphere is: ',V)
```

21. A string is a continuous sequence of a collection of characters, whose first character has the index number `0`. The length of a string can be found by using the `len()` function.

For example: `print(len("python")`

It will print 6.

Computer Application (CBSE) Code-165

Sample Question Paper 9

M.M. 30 **Time: 2 hrs**

General instructions

- **This paper contains 4 sections-Section A, Section B, Section C, and Section D.**
- **Section A and B has to be attempted by all students.**
- **Students may attempt any one of the two sections from Section C (Scratch) and Section D (Python).**

SECTION 'A' (7 Marks)

1. What happens when you click on the hyperlink? **(1)**
2. Define the forms in HTML. **(1)**
3. What does internet fraud mean? **(1)**
4. What does a blog refer to? **(1)**

OR

Mr. John has a prepaid internet connection, where he has a data limit of 14 GB. The average size of e-mail attachments that he can download is 1.4 MB. Approximately, how many e-mails can john download without exceeding his data limit?

5. Write down the examples of freeware software. **(1)**
6. Chinky has to send an e-mail to Komal. She also wants to send the same e-mail to Palvi but does not want Komal to know about it. Which option out of cc or bcc should Chinky use to enter the e-mail address of Palvi? **(1)**
7. What is the use of multi-use software Licenses? **(1)**

SECTION 'B' (15 Marks)

8. Laleema Chakradhar wants a broadband connection for accessing her mails and staying informed about the latest happenings in the field of

Biotechnology. Can you suggest two Internet Service Providers in India who can be approached for the same? **(2)**

9. What are the various types of plagiarism? Explain them. **(2)**

10. Identify the error(s) in the following HTML code. Also, write the correct code and underline the correction. **(2)**

```
<BODY color="red" background ="logo.jpg">
```

OR

Identify which of the following is a tag or an attribute:

a. `Align`

b. `Border`

c. `Src`

d. `Img`

e. `Br`

11. Write the expansions of the following tags used in HTML. **(2)**

a. `<BR>`

b. `<OL>`

c. `<HR>`

d. `<DL>`

12. How can embedded style be linked with HTML documents? **(2)**

13. How to create a web page that will use a single-line text input that will be used to take name and e-mail address of a user. **(2)**

14. Create an external style sheet `style.css` with the following specifications for the various HTML tags **(3)**

```
<BODY>:
 Background color should be Aqua( )
 Foreground color should be Navy( )
<H1>
 Should be underlined and center aligned
<P>
 First line should be indented to 60px
 Font-weight should be normal
```

Write the HTML code to create a link from the HTML document to the stylesheet (`style.css`).Where, in the HTML document, should the code be placed?

OR

Observe the following image and write down its code.

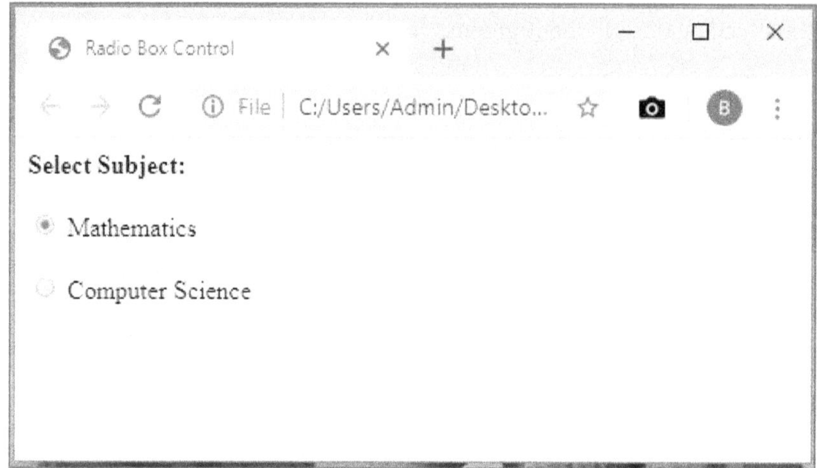

SECTION 'C' (Scratch) (8 Marks)

15. What is the purpose of using the wait instruction? Which block is used for this? **(2)**

OR

Explain the meaning of blocks?

16. Explain any three string operators and its functions. **(4)**
17. Write a script to draw a colorful circleas shown below: **(2)**

SECTION 'D' (Python) (8 Marks)

18. Explain logical operators and its types. **(2)**

19. What will be the output of the following code: **(2)**

```
a = 20
b = 10
c = 15
d = 5
e = 0

e = (a + b) * c / d        #( 30 * 15 ) / 5
print (“Value of (a + b) * c / d is “,  e)

e = ((a + b) * c) / d      # (30 * 15 ) / 5
print (“Value of ((a + b) * c) / d is “,  e)

e = (a + b) * (c / d);     # (30) * (15/5)
print (“Value of (a + b) * (c / d) is “,  e)

e = a + (b * c) / d;       #  20 + (150/5)
print (“Value of a + (b * c) / d is “,  e)
```

20. Out of the following, find those identifiers that cannot be used for naming variables and functions in a Python programming language: **(2)**

    `Roll#No, continue, True, 41stno, _v1, No_2, false, Var1`

21. Write a program to enter the temperature in Fahrenheit and convert it into centigrade. **(2)**

Answers

SECTION 'A'

1. When a user clicks on the hyperlink, he/she is navigated to the linked Web page that can be either a different Web page or a section on the same Web page or a different Web page.

2. Forms are the means to collect the user information, whenever a user fills any form or provides any details, and then save it into the database.

3. Internet fraud is a type of fraud or deception that uses the internet for tricking victims for money, property.

4. A blog is an online journal or a personal diary, where an individual writes his/her thoughts about a specific topic, posts some write-ups, and shares his/her views.

OR

10000 mails

5. An example of freeware software is Internet Explorer, and Microsoft web browser.

6. bcc (blind carbon copy).

7. This license allows us to install a program onto multiple computers, used by multiple users.

SECTION 'B'

8. VSNL and Airtel.
(Answer may vary)

9. The various types of plagiarism are:

   a. Direct plagiarism: Direct plagiarism is the word-for-word transcription of a section of someone else's work, without attribution and without quotation marks.

   b. Self-plagiarism: Self-plagiarism occurs when a student submits his or her own previous work, or mixes parts of previous works, without permission from all the professors involved.

   c. Mosaic plagiarism: Mosaic Plagiarism occurs when a student borrows phrases from a source without using quotation marks or finds synonyms for the author's language while retaining the same general structure and the meaning of the original.

   d. Accidental plagiarism: Accidental plagiarism occurs when a person neglects to cite their sources, or mis-quotes their sources, or unintentionally paraphrases a source by using similar words, groups of words, and/or sentence structure, without attribution.

10. The error is that we use bgcolor attribute in place of color.

```
<BODY bgcolor ="red" background ="logo.jpg">
```

OR

a. Attribute

b. Attribute

c. Attribute

d. Tag

e. Tag

11. *a.* Break

b. Ordered list

c. Horizontal rule

d. Definition list

12. Embedded style can be implemented within an HTML code. It is written using the `<Style>` tag and used under the `<Head>` structure.

The syntax of it is as follows:

```
<Head>
<Style Type= "Text/Css">
Style {Text-Indent: 15pt;}
Style1{Text-Color: #060000;}
</Style>
</Head>
```

13. Refer to the following code:

```
<html>
<head>
<title> Textbox control</title>
</head>
<form method="post">
Name: <INPUT type="text" name="firstname" size=20 maxlength=100 >
<BR><BR>
Email: <input name="text" type="text" name="email" size=20 max-
length=100 >
</form>
</body>
</html>
```

14. Refer to the following code:

```
"style.css"
body
{
background-color: Aqua;
color:navy
}
h1
{
text-align:center;
text-decoration:underline;
}
p
{
font-weight:normal;
text-indent:60px;
}
```

To create a link from the HTML document to the style sheet (`style.css`), the following code will be inserted in the header section of the HTML code, that is, between the `<head>` and the `</head>` tags.

```
<link href="style.css" rel ="stylesheet" type="text/css">
```

OR

Refer to the following code:

```
<html>
<head>
<title>Radio Box Control</title>
</head>
<body>
<form>
<b>Select Subject:</b><BR><BR>
<input type="radio"name="subject" value="maths" checked> Mathe-
matics
<BR>
<BR>
```

```
<input type="radio"name="subject" value="cs"> Computer Science
</form>
</body>
</html>
```

SECTION 'C' (Scratch)

15. The WAIT instruction is needed to slow down the acting, so that we can see or hear it properly. We can get the wait instruction from the CONTROL menu.

OR

Blocks are commands or instructions or lines, which are used to create a script by dragging the block onto a script area. We can create more than one script for a script area, and each script can have as many blocks as we need.

16. *a.* join hello world : It concatenates (combines) strings.

b. letter 1 of world : It reports the letter at the specified position in a string.

c. length of world : It reports the number of letters in a string.

17.

```
when [flag] clicked
go to x: 0 y: 0
clear
pen down
set pen color to 20
repeat 360
    move 1 steps
    turn ↺ 1 degrees
    change pen color by 1
```

SECTION 'D' (Python)

18. Logical operators are used to combine one or more conditions or expressions. The various logical operators are: Unary! (`NOT`) and Binary `||(OR)`, `&&` `(AND)`. While using logical operators, the expression always results into true or false that is, 1 or 0, depending upon the combination of the logical operators used.

Types of logical operators:

Operator	Description	Example
and (Logical AND)	If both the operands are true, then the condition becomes true.	(a and b) is true.
or (Logical OR)	If any of the two operands are non-zero, then the condition becomes true.	(a or b) is true.
not (Logical NOT)	Used to reverse the logical state of its operand.	Not(a and b) is false.

19. The following will be the output:

```
90.0
90.0
90.0
50.0
```

20. Roll#No, Continue, True

21. Refer to the following code:

```
f=int(input("Enter the temperature in centigrade : "))
c=(f-32)*5
print("The temperature in Fahrenheit is :is: ",c)
```

Revise Scratch Programming

Go to: https://qrgo.page.link/z9L2r Or Scan: 

Computer Application (CBSE) Code-165

Sample Question Paper 10

M.M. 30 **Time: 2 hrs**

General instructions

- **This paper contains 4 sections-Section A, Section B, Section C, and Section D.**
- **Section A and B has to be attempted by all students.**
- **Students may attempt any one of the two sections from Section C (Scratch) and Section D (Python).**

SECTION 'A' (7 Marks)

1. What is a Newsgroup? **(1)**
2. What is the extension of HTML documents? **(1)**
3. What is the meaning of product key? **(1)**
4. Name any three services provided on the Internet. **(1)**

OR

What is the use of blogs?

5. Write down the examples of free software. **(1)**
6. What is the use of mobile technology? **(1)**
7. What do you mean by Site license? **(1)**

SECTION 'B' (15 Marks)

8. What is VTC? How does it take place? **(2)**
9. Explain the various threats to digital property. **(2)**
10. Write down the following with respect to an ordered list? **(2)**

a. What is the purpose of using the 'type' and 'start'attributes?

   b. Write down its syntax.

11. How to create a web page that will show the spanning of rows and columns in a table.

Note: Use `cellspacing` and `cellpadding` attribute. **(2)**

OR

Observe the following code and write down its output:

```
<HTML>
<HEAD>
<TITLE>HTML font Tag</TITLE>
</HEAD>
<BODY>
<h2>Unordered List with Square Bullet</h2>
<ul type="square">
<li>Pizza</li>
<li>Burger</li>
<li>Noodles</li>
</ul>
<h2>Unordered List with Disc Bullet</h2>
<ul type="disc">
<li>Coke</li>
<li>Fanta</li>
<li>Dew</li>
</ul>
<h2>Unordered List with Circle Bullet</h2>
<ul type="circle">
<li>Hot Tea</li>
<li>Ice Tea</li>
<li>Coffee</li>
</ul>
</BODY>
</HTML>
```

12. Answer the following with respect to HTML: **(2)**

    a. Which tag produces a Horizontal line spread across the width of the browser window?

    b. Which tag provides a single line space between two lines?

13. Observe the following screenshot and write down its HTML code. **(2)**

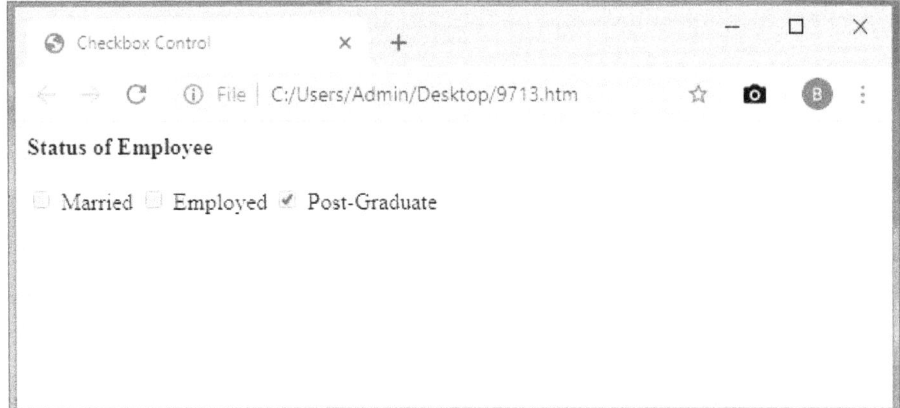

14. What is text transformation? What are the possible values it can have? **(3)**

OR

Observe the following code and write down its output:

```
<HTML>
<HEAD>
<TITLE>USE OF BR TAG</TITLE>
</HEAD>
<BODY
I WANDERED lonely as a cloud <BR>
That floats on high o'er vales and hills,<BR>
When all at once I saw a crowd,<BR>
A host, of golden daffodils;<BR>
Beside the lake, beneath the trees,<BR>
Fluttering and dancing in the breeze.<BR>
</BODY>
</HTML>
```

SECTION 'C' (Scratch) (8 Marks)

15. Name the different types of blocks in scratch. **(2)**

OR

Explain blocks palette with example.

16. Explain the looks block and its five functions. **(4)**

17. How to make a colorful circle in scratch. **(2)**

SECTION 'D' (Python) (8 Marks)

18. Explain assignment operators and its types. **(2)**

19. Rewrite the following code after underlining each correction. **(2)**

```
a=int(input("Enter the number"))
if a>10
print ("ok")
else
print ("oops")
```

20. Write a program to enter the salary of an employee and provide him a 10% commission on the salary. Calculate the net salary. **(2)**

21. Write down the output of the following program: **(2)**

```
alpha=['A','B','C','D','E','F','G','H']
for num in range(-6,-3,2):
    print(alpha[num])
```

Answers

SECTION 'A'

1. Newsgroup is an online bulletin board, where people interact with each other and share their opinions on a specific topic.
2. The HTML documents/files are saved with the extension `.HTML` or `.htm`.
3. It is the method of providing an authentication to our product. While purchasing the application, the user would be provided with a product key, which he/she would have to put while installing the application.

4. The internet provides various services that are as diverse as the internet itself. Some of these services are as follows:

   a. Email

   b. Search engines

   c. Chatting

   (Answer may vary)

OR

Blogs allow the users to edit, update, or delete the post as per requirement.

5. Examples of free software are Linux kernel, Python 3.7.3, Java Net Beans IDE, MYSQL, Apache tomcat server, and openoffice.org office suite.

6. Mobile technology is a wireless communication technology to send and receive information through Wi-Fi, broadband connection, or virtual private networks.

7. This license allows a program to be installed on an unlimited number of computers, with an unlimited number of users, if they are at the location of the site license. Site licenses are usually for schools and businesses.

SECTION 'B'

8. The full form of VTC is Video conferencing or Video Tele Conference, which represents a real-life meeting environment. It has brought the world much closer than it was before. With the help of the VTC facility, we can see other people while talking to them.

   A camera takes the video picture and also records the associated audio. The picture and the audio signal are converted into compressed digital signals. These converted audio and video signals are transmitted through a modem to the other end, where they are converted back into the picture and audio, which is projected on the screen and heard through the speakers.

9. Threats to digital properties are as follows:

   a. Phishing: Phishing is the method of stealing the username and password to get access to the system illegally. This allows attackers to take advantage of a user's public information (via social networks) to perform frauds with increased authenticity.

   b. Code hacking: Some developers conduct a plagiarism attack and steal the source code of our work and mark them as their own.

c. Sharing of data: Some users intentionally share some other user's creativity, music or artwork on social media, without seeking permission from the owner, which is also a serious digital threat.

10. a. The type attribute specifies the type of numbers or bullets, depending on whether the list item is inside an ordered list or unordered list.

The size attribute is used to change the beginning value of an ordered list. Normally, the ordered list begins with 1. It lets us customize an HTML ordered list further, by setting a new starting digit or alphabet for the ordered list element.

b. Syntax:

```
<OL start=”value” type = “value”>
```

11. Refer to the following code:

```
<HTML>
<head>
<title>Cellpadding and Cellspacing  Attribute </title>
</head>
<body>
<table border=2 cellspacing=10 cellpadding=20>
<tr>
<th>Employee code </th>
<th>Basic Salary</th>
</tr>
<tr>
<td>EM001</td>
<td>10000</td>
</tr>
<tr>
<td>EM002</td>
<td>10500</td>
</tr>
</table>

</body>
</HTML>
```

OR

Unordered List with Square Bullet

- Pizza
- Burger
- Noodles

Unordered List with Disc Bullet

- Coke
- Fanta
- Dew

Unordered List with Circle Bullet

- Hot Tea
- Ice Tea
- Coffee

12. *a.* <HR>

b.

13. Refer to the following code:

```
<html>
<head>
<title>Checkbox Control</title>
</head>
<body>
<form>
<b>Status of Employee</b><br><br>
<input type=”checkbox”name=”married”value=”on”> Married
<input type=”checkbox”name=”Employed”value=”on”> Employed
<input type=”checkbox”name=”post graduate”value=”on” checked>
Post-Graduate
</form>
</body>
</html>
```

14. The text-transform property controls the case of a text. The various values it can have are:

a. Capitalize: It capitalizes the first letter of each word. For example: `computer applications` will be displayed as `Computer Applications`.

b. Uppercase: Converts all the letters to uppercase. For example: `computer applications` will be displayed as `COMPUTER APPLICATIONS`.

c. Lowercase: Converts all the letters to lowercase. For example: `COMPUTER APPLICATIONS` will be displayed as `computer applications`.

d. None: No transformations - the text is presented as it appears in the HTML code.

OR

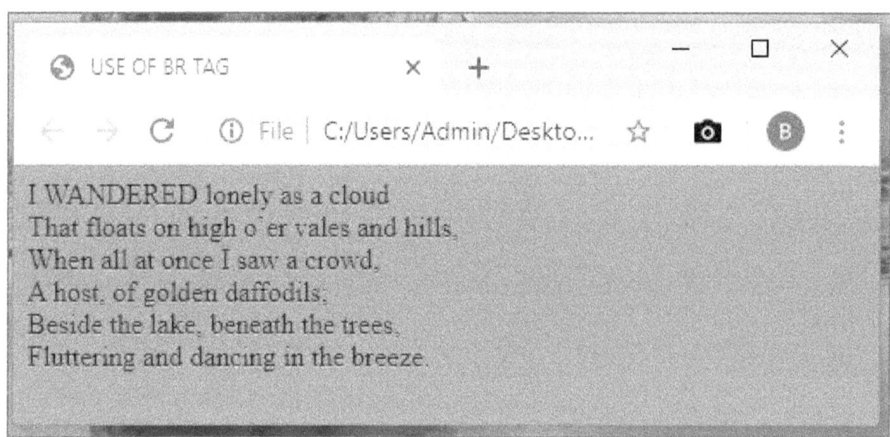

SECTION 'C' (Scratch)

15. The different types of blocks available in scratch are: Motion blocks, Looks blocks, Sound blocks, Pen blocks, Data blocks, Events blocks, Control blocks, Sensing blocks, Operator blocks and more blocks (user created blocks).

OR

The blocks palette contains the blocks that we can use to make our scripts. Each block represents one instruction in our program. For example, we can give instructions for moving, rotating or playing the sprite on a stage. The blocks in the palette are divided into several categories such as motion, events, control, sensing, operators, data, look, and more. The instructions on the blocks in the stack create a script or a program. The instructions on all the blocks get executed when we click anywhere on the stack.

16. Looks blocks control how our sprites and the backdrop will look. They also control the size of the sprite and whether the sprites are displayed in the front or behind the stage or script pane. These blocks are in purple color. The looks blocks also include blocks that let you display text.

BLOCK	FUNCTION
say Hello! for 2 secs	Makes a time-limited speech balloon appear above the selected sprite.
say Hello!	Makes a persistent speech balloon appear above the selected sprite.
think Hmm... for 2 secs	Makes a time-limited thought balloon appear above the selected sprite.
think Hmm...	Makes a persistent thought balloon appear above the selected sprite.
show	Displays the sprite immediately.

17.

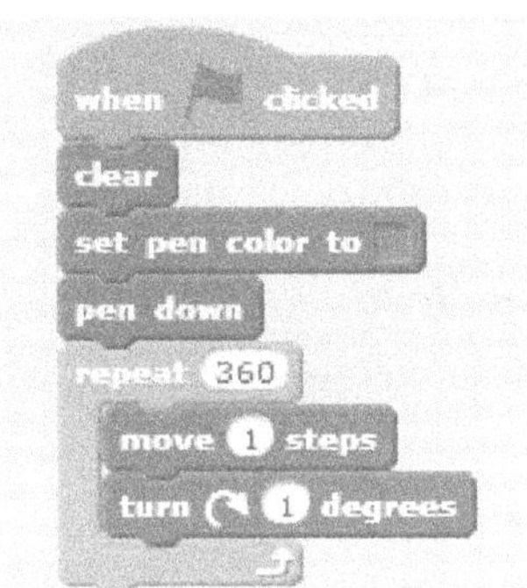

To make a green color circle,

a. Set the pen color to Green.

b. Pen must be in drawing position.

c. Repeat the following commands 360 times:

i. Move 1 step.

ii. Turn 1 degree.

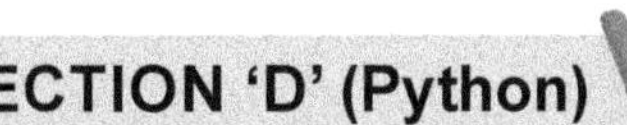

SECTION 'D' (Python)

18. The assignment operators are used to assign values of the right expression to the left operand. They perform simple arithmetic operations and are also known as 'augmented operators'.

Operator	Description	Example
=	Assigns values from right side operands to the left side operand.	c = a + b assigns value of a + b into c
+= Add	It adds the right operand to the left operand and assigns the result to the left operand.	c += a is equivalent to c = c + a
-= Subtract	It subtracts the right operand from the left operand and assigns the result to the left operand.	c -= a is equivalent to c = c - a
*= Multiply	It multiplies the right operand with the left operand and assigns the result to the left operand.	c *= a is equivalent to c = c * a
/= Divide	It divides the left operand with the right operand and assigns the result to the left operand.	c /= a is equivalent to c = c/ ac /= a is equivalent to c =c / a
%= Modulus	It takes the modulus using two operands and assigns the result to the left operand.	c %= a is equivalent to c = c% a
**= Exponent	Performs exponential (power) calculation on the operators and assignsthe value to the left operand.	c **= a is equivalent to c = c** a

19. Refer to the following code:

```
a=int(input("Enter the number"))
if a>10:
print ("ok")
else
print ("oops")
```

20. Refer to the following code:

```
sal=int(input("Enter salary : "))
com=sal*0.10
net=sal+com
print("Net Salary = ",net)
```

21. The following will be the output:

```
C
E
G
```

Self
Assessment

Computer Application (CBSE) Code-165

Self Assessment 1

M.M. 30 **Time: 2 hrs**

General instructions

- **This paper contains 4 sections-Section A, Section B, Section C, and Section D.**
- **Section A and B has to be attempted by all students.**
- **Students may attempt any one of the two sections from Section C (Scratch) and Section D (Python).**

SECTION 'A' (7 Marks)

1. Explain MMS. **(1)**
2. Write down the properties of Margin in CSS. **(1)**
3. How many versions of GPL are available? **(1)**
4. What happens when the receiver's mobile is off or not in the network area when the message is sent? **(1)**

   OR

   Write down one disadvantage of online shopping.
5. What is the purpose of the SET protocol? **(1)**
6. Name the folder in which e-mail messages are stored. **(1)**
7. What is the use of a digital signature? **(1)**

SECTION 'B' (15 Marks)

8. Muneesh's head office is in USA and he lives in Noida. His office has other branches in UK, Canada and Singapore. He often uses video conferencing to connect with other branch managers and take updates. **(2)**

   a. List two advantages of him using video conferencing.

   b. List two problems that he could face while video conferencing.

9. How can you protect your data and identity, while selling and buying products online? **(2)**

10. Write the HTML program that makes the body text appear 60 pixels away from the top edge of the page and 75 pixels away from the left edge of the page. **(2)**

11. Answer the following with respect to HTML: **(2)**

    a. What is the use of the `<font>` tag?

    b. What are the attributes of the `<font>` tag?

    Not to forget: HTML is not a case sensitive language. So, you can write <FONT> tag this one as well.

    OR

    Write down the output of the following code:

```
<HTML>
<HEAD>
<TITLE>Ordered List </TITLE>
</HEAD>
<BODY>
<ol>
<li> Breakfast</li>
<li> Lunch </li>
</ol>
</BODY>
</HTML>
```

12. Observe the following table and write the HTML code to generate it: **(2)**

Marks			
English	**Maths**	**Economics**	**Physics**
67	89	77	92

Note: 1st row has a yellow background and the 2nd row has green background.

Solution hints: In this code, you use <caption> tag and bgcolor.

13. Consider the following code and find the output: **(2)**

```
<HTML>
<HEAD>
<TITLE> My First Stylesheet </TITLE>
<STYLE TYPE = "text/css">
H1 {color : green; font-size : 37px; font-family : impact}
P {text-indent : 1cm; background : yellow}
</STYLE>
</HEAD>
<BODY>
<H1> Stylesheets : The Tool of the Web Design Gods </H1>
<P> Amaze your friends! Squash your enemies! </P>
</BODY>
</HTML>
```

14. Write the HTML code to generate the following form. Save it as `task1.html`. **(3)**

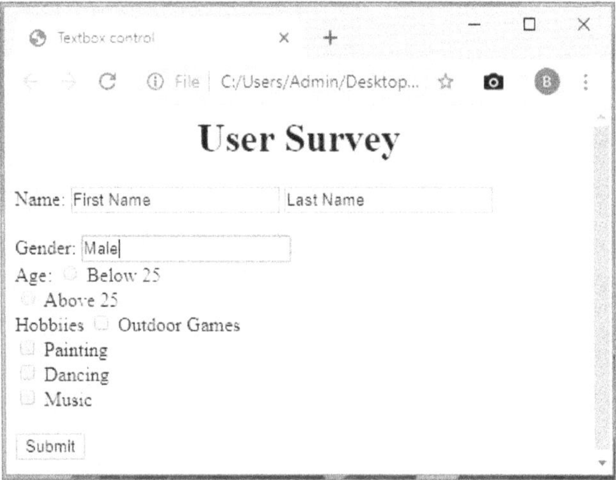

OR

Write the CSS code to:

a. Apply `50px` indentation to all the text paragraphs marked with `<p>`.

b. Make the text *italics*, in the paragraphs marked with the `<p>` tag.

SECTION 'C' (Scratch) (8 Marks)

15. Define the purpose of the motion block and the costume block. **(2)**

OR

Differentiate between the repeat block and the repeat until block.

16. Write a scratch program to draw the mathematical shapes like square and triangle, using the Pen Block. **(4)**

17. Explain the following: **(2)**

a. Script Area

b. Green Flag

SECTION 'D' (Python) (8 Marks)

18. Write any four features of Python. **(2)**

19. Analyze the following code andwrite down its output. **(2)**

```
Even = False
If Even:
    Print ("It is even!")
```

20. What does the following statement mean? **(2)**

```
a,b,c=1,1.2,"John"
```

21. Write a program to compute the total cost, where the user inputs number of units and price per unit. **(2)**

Computer Application (CBSE) Code-165

Self Assessment 2

M.M. 30 **Time: 2 hrs**

General instructions

- **This paper contains 4 sections-Section A, Section B, Section C, and Section D.**
- **Section A and B has to be attempted by all students.**
- **Students may attempt any one of the two sections from Section C (Scratch) and Section D (Python).**

SECTION 'A' (7 Marks)

1. What is the purpose of a newsgroup? **(1)**
2. Give an example of the container tag in HTML. **(1)**
3. What is the meaning of SSL? **(1)**
4. What categories are E-banking divided into? **(1)**

   OR

   How one can move from one web page to another?
5. Write down one advantage of Intellectual Property Rights. **(1)**
6. Expand FTP. **(1)**
7. What is the use of Proprietary software? **(1)**

SECTION 'B' (15 Marks)

8. A school has two separate computer networks. One is used for keeping the pupil and staff records. The other is for pupils to use in lessons, to help with their learning, and to store their work. **(2)**
9. What is the difference between direct plagiarism and self-plagiarism? **(2)**
10. Answer the following with respect to HTML: **(2)**
    a. Name the tag that is used to create a hyperlink.

b. Name the attribute that is used to set the color for the visited links in a web page.

11. Consider the following CSS code: **(2)**

```
h1 {font-family: arial, comic sans-serif, "Times New Roman";}
```

Explain the font-family.

12. Write the names of two attributes for each tag: **(2)**

a. <HR>

b. <Body>

c. <img>

d. <Table>

13. Write the code to create the following HTML Form to accept the User's Information as a part of a Magazine Survey: **(2)**

Note: Address accepts multi-line text.

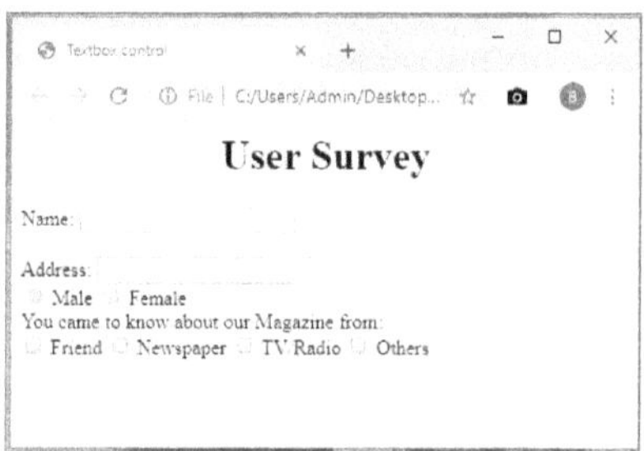

14. Observe the following code and find the output: **(3)**

```
<HTML>
<body>
</p>
<form name="form1" method="post" action=" ">
<p>Outdoor Games You Play</p>
<p>
<input type="checkbox" name="game1" value="table tennis"> Table
Tennis<br>
<br>
<input type="checkbox" name="game2" value="football">Foot
Ball<br>
<br>
<input type="checkbox" name="game3" value="swimming">Swimming<br>
<br>
```

```
</p>
</form></form>
</body>
<html>
```

OR

What is the difference between the subscript and superscript tags used in HTML? Also, give one program to illustrate the same.

SECTION 'C' (Scratch) (8 Marks)

15. What is the meaning of a sensing block? **(2)**

OR

What is the purpose of the events block in scratch?

16. Write a program in scratch to draw a pentagon, without using the repeat block. **(4)**

Solution hints: In pentagon, you will use 5 times move and point in direction block.

17. What is the difference between the script area and script? **(2)**

SECTION 'D' (Python) (8 Marks)

18. Write down the rules for identifying the identifiers. **(2)**

19. Write down the output of the following code: **(2)**

```
Age = int (input ("Enter age"))
If age>18:
    print ("Eligible for vote")
```

20. Write a program in Python to display the sum of the first n natural numbers. **(2)**

OR

Write a program in Python to display the sum of all the digits of a number.

Not to forget: In some versions of python, brackets are optional. If you do not want to use brackets in print, your code will be not be wrong.

21. Find the errors in following code: **(2)**

```
i= 0;
While i<3:
print ('hi', end = '')
    print ('bye', end = '')
    i = i + 1;
print ('bye')
```

Computer Application (CBSE) Code-165

Self Assessment 3

M.M. 30 **Time: 2 hrs**

General instructions

- **This paper contains 4 sections-Section A, Section B, Section C, and Section D.**
- **Section A and B has to be attempted by all students.**
- **Students may attempt any one of the two sections from Section C (Scratch) and Section D (Python).**

SECTION 'A' (7 Marks)

1. Write down one advantage of email. **(1)**
2. What is the function of the <body> tag? **(1)**
3. What protocols have been developed for Visa and MasterCard? **(1)**
4. Write down one disadvantage of MMS. **(1)**

   OR

   What are the services of Mobile banking?
5. What are the advantages of e-commerce? (*Any two*) **(1)**
6. What is the purpose of 'To' in an e-mail structure? **(1)**
7. What is PCI? **(1)**

SECTION 'B' (15 Marks)

8. Pupils use the internet frequently in their lessons to help them with their work. Discuss the advantages and disadvantages of this pertaining to the pupil. **(2)**
9. Write down the rules that you need to follow, while communicating online. **(2)**

   Solution hints: Do not disclose your personal information online.
10. Write down the following with respect to CSS: **(2)**

   a. Name the property that specifies an extra line around the content.

   b. Name the property that is used to display a particular type of border on an HTML document.

11. How can you set the left and the right side margin of a web page? **(2)**

12. Observe the following code carefully and answer the questions that follow: **(2)**

The Dos and Don'ts of network security

```
KEEP ANTI-VIRUS SOFTWARE UP TO DATE.
SAVE THE FILE TO COMPUTER OR A DISK.
RUN AN ANTI-VIRUS SCAN REGULARLY.
```

Predict the output of the above code, while explaining the effects applied in the CSS code.

OR

Carefully read and answer the following questions with respect to HTML:

   a. What does a Form consist of?

   b. Which tag is used to insert a Form in an HTML document? Is it a container or a non-container tag?

13. Write the HTML code to send an email to `abc@xyz.com` through your webpage. **(2)**

14. How can you provide space between letters? Explain with a suitable example. **(3)**

OR

Write output of the following HTML code:

```
<html><head><title> Table </title></head>
<body>
<table border="1">
<tr><th align="center" rowspan="3"> ONE </th><th> TWO </th>
<th>THREE </th></tr>
<tr><td> Rose </td><td> Lily </td></tr>
<tr><td align="center"> Pansy </td><td align="center"
colspan="2"> Dahlia </td></tr>
</table>
```

```
</body>
</html>
```

SECTION 'C' (Scratch) (8 Marks)

15. What is the purpose of a variable in Scratch? **(2)**

OR

What is the use of the if condition? Explain with an example.

16. Write a program in scratch to draw a hexagon using the repeat block. **(4)**

17. Which is the block that is used to perform various mathematical operations? **(2)**

SECTION 'D' (Python) (8 Marks)

18. What are literals and its types? **(2)**

19. Write down the output of the following code: **(2)**

```
fruits = ["Palvi","Nishi","Kartik","Ashay","Chinky"]
    print (type(names))
    for name in names:
        print(name)
```

20. How many times are the following loops executed? **(2)**

```
i=200
while(i<=300):
    print i
    i+=30
```

Not to forget: Loop is a sequence of instructions that are repeated until a certain specified condition is met.

21. Write a program in Python to display the surface area of a cylinder. **(2)**

Computer Application (CBSE) Code-165

Self Assessment 4

M.M. 30 **Time: 2 hrs**

General instructions

- **This paper contains 4 sections-Section A, Section B, Section C, and Section D.**
- **Section A and B has to be attempted by all students.**
- **Students may attempt any one of the two sections from Section C (Scratch) and Section D (Python).**

SECTION 'A' (7 Marks)

1. Write down the features of the 4G technology. (*Any two*) **(1)**
2. What is the syntax of the `<p>` tag in HTML? **(1)**
3. What are workstation licenses? **(1)**
4. Write down two disadvantages of blogging. **(1)**

   OR

   What is the purpose of a social networking site?
5. What is FLOSS? **(1)**
6. What is the difference between a website and a webpage? **(1)**
7. What is encrypting and decrypting of data? **(1)**

SECTION 'B' (15 Marks)

8. Identify the domain names and URLs from the following list: **(2)**

   a. `abc@abc.com`

   b. `doyogaeveryday.com`

   d. `www.doyogaeveryday.com/index.html`

   e. `192.168.0.1`

9. What is software license and what are its various types? **(2)**

10. Observe the following table and write the HTML code to generate it: **(2)**

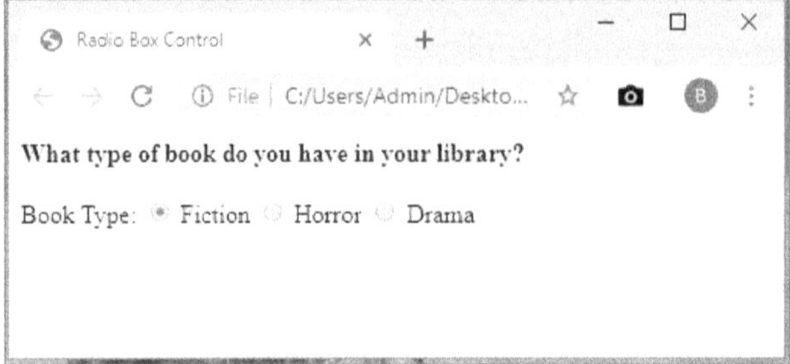

Solution hints: In this code, you use <h2> tag.

11. Write the HTML code to do the following: **(2)**

    a. To display a horizontal line of green color.

    b. To create a hyperlink on the word 'CLICK', to an image named `testimage.jpeg`.

12. Can you set the height and the width of an image? If yes, then how? Give an example to illustrate the same. **(2)**

13. Write the name of the tag used for the following: **(2)**

    a. Inserting images

    b. Inserting an external and internal link

OR

Observe the following screenshot and write down its code:

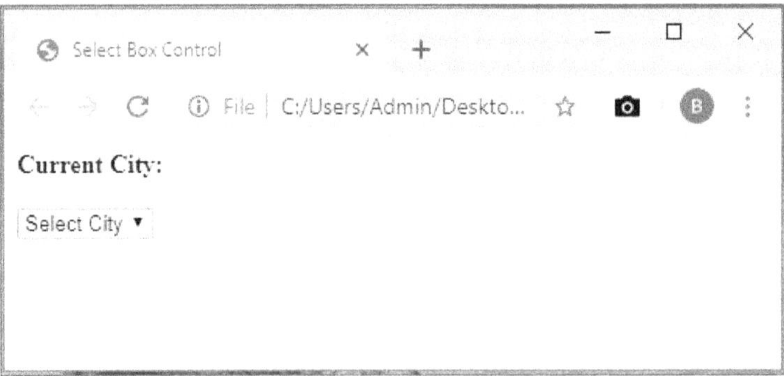

14. Carefully observe the following, labeled screenshot and answer the questions that follow: **(3)**

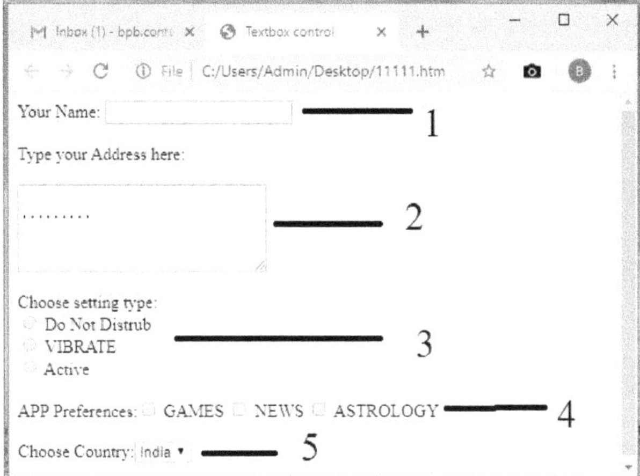

a. Identify the form element labeled as 1 and 2.

b. What has the form element labeled as 2 used to input the Address?

c. Write the HTML code to create the form element labeled 3.

d. Differentiate between the form element labeled 3 and the form element labeled 4.

e. How can any one item be highlighted in the dropdown box be labeled as 5?

OR

Observe the following screenshot and write down its HTML code:

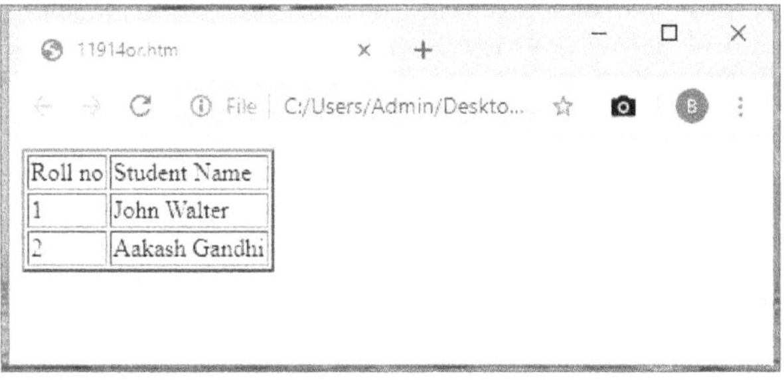

SECTION 'C' (Scratch) **(8 Marks)**

15. Explain the types of cursor tools available in scratch. **(2)**

OR

What are tabs and its types?

16. Draw a square using therepeat block of commands. **(4)**

Not to forget: For any shapes, turn angle will 360/number of slides.

17. Write a program in scratch to input say Hello. **(2)**

SECTION 'D' (Python) (8 Marks)

18. How many types of comments are available in Python? **(2)**

19. Identify the following identifiers: **(2)**

```
11 name, salary 13, gross_salary, ?Palvi, @Komal
```

20. What will be the output of the following code? **(2)**

```
a = 1
while a<=5:
    print(a)
    a+=1
    print ("End")
```

21. Write a program in Python to find the largest number out of the three numbers. **(2)**

Computer Application (CBSE) Code-165

Self Assessment 5

M.M. 30 **Time: 2 hrs**

General instructions

- **This paper contains 4 sections-Section A, Section B, Section C, and Section D.**
- **Section A and B has to be attempted by all students.**
- **Students may attempt any one of the two sections from Section C (Scratch) and Section D (Python).**

SECTION 'A' (7 Marks)

1. What is an email address? **(1)**
2. What are the attributes of the horizontal rule? **(1)**

   Not to forget: Horizontal rule is same as horizontal rule attribute.
3. Name some common intellectual property rights. **(1)**
4. Write down two disadvantages of E-reservation. **(1)**

   OR

   Explain the functioning of the FTP and SFTP.
5. What is copyright? **(1)**
6. List the different domain extensions. **(1)**
7. What are cyber netiquettes? **(1)**

SECTION 'B' (15 Marks)

8. Identify the web addresses and email addresses from the following: **(2)**

   a. `www.scrapbook.com`

   b. `aba@crapbook.com`

   c. `www.countrywide.co.in`

   d. `123@hotshot.co.in`

9. Write any two precautions that should be taken while using the internet. **(2)**

10. Write the full form of the following: **(2)**

    a. <P>

    b. <UL>

    c. <LI>

    d. SRC

11. Write the HTML code to display an image on the RIGHT side of the page. **(2)**

    OR

    How you will nest an unordered list inside an ordered list?

12. Write a code in HTML to insert an image where the alternate text is set by using the altattribute. **(2)**

    Solution hints: <P> is a container tag whereas <BR> is an empty tag.

13. Distinguish between the <P> tag and the <BR> tag, with the help of an example. **(2)**

14. Observe the following web page and write the HTML code to generate it: **(3)**

Note the following points while generating the Webpage:

The link color is black, the background color is yellow and the visited link color is green.

- Title of the page is `Online Shopping`.
- Heading of the page is Red.
- Caption of table is blue.
- Table border is blue and of size 2.
- The 4 links are `one.html`, `two.html`, `three.html` and `four.html`.
- The email id for 'contact us' is `abc@xyz.com`.

OR

What will be the output of the following code?

```
<HTML>
<HEAD>
<TITLE>HTML ordered list tag</TITLE>
</HEAD>
<BODY>
<h3>A numbered list with start value 1:</h3>
<OL start=1>
<li>Apple</li>
<li>Mango</li>
<li>Banana</li>
<li>Strawberry</li>
</ol>
<h3>An alphabetized list with start value 2:</h3>
<ol type="A" start=2>
<li>Red</li>
<li>Blue</li>
<li>Orange</li>
<li>Pink</li>
</OL>
</BODY>
</HTML>
```

SECTION 'C' (Scratch) (8 Marks)

15. What is a sprite list? (2)

OR

What is the use of a title bar in scratch?

16. Explain the ask and answer blocks in detail. (2)

17. What is the meaning of 10 in the block `move 10 steps` and `if on edge, bounce` ? (2)

SECTION 'D' (Python) (8 Marks)

18. What is the precedence of operators? (2)

19. What will be the output of following code? (2)

```
print("eat every day.")
print("eat healthy.")
```

20. Find the error from the following code: (2)

```
a=Kanika
b=Nishi
Print a+b
```

21. Write a program in Python to check if the input number is prime or not. (2)

www.ingramcontent.com/pod-product-compliance
Ingram Content Group UK Ltd.
Pitfield, Milton Keynes, MK11 3LW, UK
UKHW061655190726
13853UKWH00008B/2219